GOD ANSWERS OUR PRAYERS

TRUE STORIES OF GOD'S POWER AND PROMISE

CHRISTIAN WRITERS FOR LIFE

CONTENTS

INTRODUCTION

In life's most trying moments, when fear and uncertainty cloud our way, the power of prayer has the ability to shine through, bringing hope, healing, and peace. *God Answers Our Prayers* is a collection of true stories that explore the profound impact prayer can have on our lives. Each story invites readers into a unique personal experience—whether it's a miraculous healing, protection from harm, provision in times of need, or an encounter with God's love in moments of deep despair.

These testimonies come from people just like you—individuals who have faced challenges, heartache, and moments of desperate need, only to find that prayer truly changes things. Through prayers of faith, they have witnessed God's answers and miraculous interventions in the form of divine healings, life-changing encounters, and even the subtle but undeniable whisper of His presence.

The purpose of this book is to encourage, inspire, and uplift readers, reminding them that God is near, that He hears their prayers, that He answers their prayers, and that no request is too small or too great for Him. Whether you are in the midst of a personal storm or simply seeking to deepen your faith, *God Answers Our Prayers* will fill you with hope, strengthen your trust in God, and remind you of the power of unwavering, heartfelt prayer.

SNOW DAY PRAYER

BY KRISTY ENSOR

I enjoyed growing up in our rural East Tennessee home with its scenic views of sunsets and gently rolling hills. My childhood bedroom was graced with wallpaper adorned with tiny yellow flowers and a canopy bed layered in yellow chiffon bedding. I often prayed underneath that yellow canopy surrounded by my rag dolls, Raggedy Ann and Holly Hobbie. That's where I began developing my close relationship with Jesus.

For years as a child, I prayed a rote prayer every night before drifting off to sleep. I simply prayed, *Lord, thank you for this day. I love you, believe in you, and trust you with all my heart, soul, mind, body, and strength. Amen.* I never changed the prayer but meant every word.

It wasn't until I was in the fourth grade that my prayers became more specific. The first detailed prayer is quite memorable.

There was a big snow in the forecast. One of my best friends, Sharon, and I asked our moms if we could have a sleepover since we were expecting to be out of school the next day due to Old Man Winter. Our mothers agreed, so Sharon came over to my house. We looked forward to a snow day.

Surprisingly, my mom came in early the next morning to wake us. *Why is Mom waking us up?* Sharon and I were stunned—we were having to go to school. We quickly got out of bed to look out the cold window. To our disappointment, there was no snow. Not one single flake in sight.

Well, that just couldn't be. What were two nine-year-old girls to do? We decided to sit back on the bed to pray. Sharon and I held hands and began praying for snow. After we prayed, we were giddy, just knowing God would answer our prayer.

Several minutes later, Mom returned with good news. "Girls, you can play some before school. The radio announcer said you're on a snow schedule." That meant we'd go to school an hour later than normal. When we looked out the window this time, it was flurrying with just a hint of snow dusting the ground.

Before playing, we decided to pray a second time. Once again, we held hands and sat underneath the yellow canopy. With all the childlike faith we could muster, Sharon and I boldly prayed for a snow day with all our might. We prayed with expectancy.

In a little while, Mom returned to my room to share that we were, indeed, out of school for the day. We hurriedly looked out the window and could hardly believe our eyes. It was snowing heavily, and the ground was completely covered in a layer of white. We received our snow day! We giggled and jumped for joy because God answered our prayer, and we could play all day instead of going to school.

Sharon and I are from different church families. Two faiths and two hopefuls. We were trusting little girls who came together and prayed to God. He answered our prayer, delivering our snow day.

As I matured in my Christian walk, I realized not all prayers are answered in such record speed as ours was that frosty winter morning. I believe God rewarded us with a snow day since He delights in prayers when they are prayed with pure hearts and childlike faith.

Although Sharon and I currently live many hours apart, we still keep in touch. Our friendship spans decades, and we remain close friends despite the miles between us. We both declare we'll never forget our snow day prayer.

* * *

Kristy Ensor is a wife, mom, and award-winning author weaving stories of hope with threads of Southern charm. She has been published in several anthologies and is a regular contributor to Lifeway's *Journey* magazine. Kristy also co-wrote the devotional *Hope Is.* Find her online at kristyensor.com and on social media—@thebackroaddiva.

Questions for Personal Reflection or Group Discussion

Kristy recounts a childhood memory of praying with her best friend, Sharon, for a snow day, trusting with childlike faith that God would answer their prayer. Against all odds, their prayer was answered, and they spent the day playing in the snow. The story illustrates the beauty of simple, sincere prayers and the joy of seeing God respond, especially when prayers are offered with pure hearts and unshakable belief.

1. How does Kristy's story of childlike faith inspire you to pray with simplicity and trust, believing that God can answer even your most seemingly small requests?
2. Can you recall a time when you prayed with great expectancy, like Kristy and Sharon did, and God answered in a way that brought joy and surprise?
3. What can you learn from this story about maintaining faith, even when not all prayers are answered immediately or in the way you expect?

We pray that Kristy's story reminds you that God delights in our prayers, no matter how big or small they may seem. Praying with a pure heart and childlike faith can lead to beautiful moments of answered prayer, reinforcing the power of trust and expectancy in our relationship with God.

FROM POVERTY TO PROVISION

BY JUANITA R. WILLIAMS

$\mathcal{I}$ was trapped in a trauma-filled house and desperately wanted out. The longer I was there, the more my soul felt like it was being crushed like refuse in a trash compactor. I was dissuaded from joining the Army and had no money for college. Because I wanted to escape so badly, in my naïveté, I devised a plan.

That plan was to have a baby and apply for public assistance and public housing so I could move out. I didn't consult God about anything and never considered the consequences of having a baby before marriage. I had a short-term plan with no regard for the life I would drag into my plight.

My baby was born two weeks before I turned nineteen. Seven months later, young and inexperienced, I moved out. I knew absolutely nothing about raising a child, but I was finally free.

Or was I?

Not thinking about long-term effects, I intentionally placed us at the poverty level. I had no plan of action for my future, no goals, and no determination to do or be better until I met my future husband.

We started dating shortly after I moved out. A little over a year later, he asked a question that would change the course of my life: "Why don't you have a job?"

I was flabbergasted. I was perfectly healthy, and there was no reason I couldn't work. I had no answer. From that day forward, my mindset shifted. It was like someone entered a very dark room and turned the light on. I pondered his question for a few days and then took action.

There is an organization in my hometown called The Urban League that provides summer jobs for teens. I was not a teen anymore but decided to apply anyway and was placed at the courthouse where I worked as a clerk. I didn't own a vehicle and needed childcare, so my child and I took the bus every day until that job ended. After that job ended, I was determined not to regress, so I searched for and found a full-time job, which afforded me the opportunity to purchase my very first car.

Between poverty and provision, my child and I moved to California. I found work but eventually decided, for personal reasons, to move back to my hometown. It didn't take me long to find a job there. I was unwavering in my quest to provide for my child who deserved better than what I chose for them. Thankfully, I was able to go back to the company where I worked before moving to California. Fortunately, I was able to buy another vehicle and move out of public housing.

One morning, after taking my child to school, I was sitting on my bed, and the word *career* dropped in my spirit. I looked up and said in my heart, *Lord, I want a career.*

That very day, the Lord reminded me of the lifetime placement program my college offered to its graduates. I immediately called the college and was connected to the job placement specialist. We set an appointment and met, and I was given a referral to the Social Security Administration. I called the manager, was interviewed, and thirty-four years later, I am still with the agency.

God used a simple question to change the trajectory of my life and place me on the path He planned for me. I thank God for using my now-husband of thirty-four years to shift my mindset from poverty and propel me to provision.

* * *

Juanita R. Williams is a native of Peoria, Illinois. She is a published author and Personal Development Coach. Fulfilling her God-given assignment, she wrote her first book, *Finding Purpose After Sexual Abuse and Trauma: Living Beyond Pain and Finding My True Identity in God*, to bring healing and hope to the broken.

Questions for Personal Reflection or Group Discussion

Juanita found herself trapped in a life of poverty, having made decisions based on short-term desires without consulting God. It wasn't until her future husband asked her a simple but powerful question that her mindset shifted. That question ignited a journey from poverty to provision as God led her from public assistance to a stable career, transforming her life and her child's future.

1. How have your decisions shaped your current circumstances, and how can you invite God into your decision-making process?
2. Have you ever experienced a moment when a simple question or conversation shifted your mindset and led to positive change?
3. How does Juanita's story encourage you to trust God to provide a way out of difficult situations and place you on a better path?

We pray that Juanita's story will remind you that God can use the simplest of moments to bring about profound change in your life. May it inspire you to trust in His provision and to be open to the ways He can shift your mindset toward a future filled with hope and opportunity. Let this testimony encourage you to pursue God's plans for your life, knowing that He has a path from poverty to provision waiting for you.

3

THE MIRACULOUS SURVIVAL OF BRYAN MCGEE

BY B.E. GOODRICH

*I*n the tranquil town of Silsbee, nestled in the heart of East Texas, a remarkable story of faith and divine intervention unfolded early one fateful Saturday morning in August 1985. My mother, Cyndi, a devoted parent to two-and-a-half-year-old me, woke up with a sudden and overwhelming urge to pray for our family's safety. Little did she know that this inexplicable prompting would soon prove to be a life-saving act of God's grace.

Two days later, on August 12, my Aunt Maxine came to visit with my cousin Carrie, a lively three-year-old. As adventurous toddlers, Carrie and I wasted no time in scampering outside to play. Drawn to Aunt Maxine's parked 1978 Buick LeSabre, we clambered into the front seat, eager to take turns pretending to drive.

When my moment to take the wheel arrived, my tiny hands grasped the shifter on the steering column, inadvertently causing the car to roll backward down the slight incline of the driveway. Gripped by the fear of getting into trouble, I made a split-second decision to open the door and jump out. In a heart-stopping instant, the door knocked me off balance, and I tumbled beneath the driver's side front tire.

Time seemed to stand still as the car slowly rolled over my small body, its weight bearing down on me from my right leg to my head. Miraculously, I felt no pain, but instead, I was enveloped by a bright, comforting light that filled my vision. The car came to rest in a shallow ditch, with Carrie crying in the front seat.

My mother and Aunt Maxine had witnessed the car rolling backward through the window, initially joking about the vehicle driving itself. Their laughter quickly turned to horror as they remembered us playing outside. Racing to the scene, my mother found me standing up, crying, with sand filling my mouth. With trembling fingers, she gently cleared the debris from my face and mouth.

As she cradled me close while rushing to the hospital, my mother noticed clumps of hair falling from the back of my head, my scalp bearing the imprint of the tire's treads. A sense of dread washed over her as she realized the extent of the accident, but her faith in God's protection never wavered.

At the emergency room, I was whisked away for X-rays and examinations, leaving my mother to wait anxiously outside. The separation was frightening for me, but the medical staff worked diligently to assess my condition.

After what felt like an eternity, the doctors emerged with astonishing news: I had miraculously escaped the ordeal without any broken bones or internal bleeding. Apart from a bruised and bloody nose, a tire print spanning my back and leg, and a bald spot where the tire had slid off my head, I was virtually unscathed.

Overwhelmed with gratitude, my mother gave thanks to Jesus for answering her fervent prayers. The incredible story of my survival spread quickly, a testament to the power of faith and the unwavering love of a God who watches over His children, even in their darkest moments. The local newspaper, *The Silsbee Bee*, even published the miraculous story.

From that day forward, my mother shared our family's miraculous tale with all who would listen, inspiring others to trust in the Lord's protection and to never underestimate the strength of a mother's prayer. My story stands as a shining example of God's grace and the power of prayer, forever etched in the hearts of those who witness the extraordinary power of divine intervention.

* * *

Born and raised amidst the sweeping vistas of Texas, **B.E. Goodrich's** published narratives flow from a wellspring of unbridled imagination. Goodrich invites readers to join him on a journey of discovery, where the extraordinary can be found within the ordinary, and the true magic of storytelling resides.

Questions for Personal Reflection or Group Discussion

In a miraculous turn of events, Cyndi felt an overwhelming urge to pray for her family's safety just days before her toddler was run over by a car. Despite the terrifying incident, God protected the child from harm, with no major injuries, and Cyndi's faith in God's care was reaffirmed. This story serves as a powerful testimony of divine intervention and the importance of trusting God's guidance through prayer.

1. Have you ever experienced a moment when you felt an urgent need to pray without knowing why? How did you respond?
2. How does this story strengthen your belief in the power of prayer and God's protection?
3. How can you be more sensitive to the promptings of the Holy Spirit in your daily life?

We pray that this story will encourage you to trust in God's ever-present care and to follow His lead, even when the reasons are unclear. May Cyndi's testimony remind you that God is always watching over us and that prayer can play a powerful role in protecting and guiding our lives. Let this miraculous story inspire you to rely on God's grace and protection, especially in times of uncertainty or danger.

4

HEALING HEARTS

BY DEANN STARLING

Our eighteen-month-old daughter peeked out from under the conference room table, laughing, oblivious to the anxiety permeating the room. My husband and I sat nearby, waiting for Sidney's test results. The surgeon soon appeared and gave us life-altering news.

"Sidney's heart does not look good. She has two holes between the chambers of her heart. More disturbingly, she has a common valve instead of two valves. The surgery will be complicated. She will likely have a stroke or other deficits. Without surgery, she will not live past age nineteen."

We lowered our heads and sobbed.

When the shock subsided, we called our families and church for prayer. We had joined our church recently and were only hoping to be added to the prayer list. Imagine our surprise when the members not only decided to fast for Sidney, but also devoted an entire Sunday service to anoint her with oil and pray.

As my husband and I held our only child at the front of that little church, my tears flowed uncontrollably—not just for Sidney, but for the outpouring of God's love unfolding in front of me.

Every person in the church touched our daughter with outstretched hands and begged God for a miracle.

Those prayers didn't stop. This was 2001, before the days of social media, yet I could go to the grocery store and complete strangers would tell me they had been praying for Sidney. Our church may have only had one hundred members, but they could rival the reach of any social media influencer today!

Months later, after much research and diligent prayer, we flew to Boston Children's Hospital for a second opinion. Before we left, our church presented us with handmade gifts and a check for $1,500. We were stunned, especially since these friends barely knew us.

Once again, we met with doctors and braced ourselves.

The cardiologist got right to the point. "Your daughter's heart does have two holes, but, contrary to the other reports, we don't see a common valve. We will patch the holes and repair her mitral valve. This is an easy surgery."

We couldn't wait to let our church know that part of their prayers had already been answered. The prognosis looked better already!

We asked our friends to pray for specific requests: a short surgery time, no need for blood transfusions, an uneventful recovery, and medical help on the return flight.

Three hours after the surgery began, the doctor announced, "We completed the surgery in record time, without blood transfusions!"

Three days later, that doctor discharged Sidney from the hospital. We kept the phone lines busy relaying every answered prayer.

Before leaving the hospital, we received the bill for the surgery. I sat stunned as I read the amount: $1,500. Exactly what our church had given us.

When we headed for the airport, Sidney looked great, but I kept praying for a medical person to be on board. Four ladies began talking to us at the gate, and, without knowing my request, said they were pediatric nurses. Almost offhandedly, one of them added, "And I'm a pediatrician."

God provided exactly who I needed.

Today, our daughter is a young adult, perfectly healthy. She has graduated from college and worked in ministry organizations, but I tell her that she even had a ministry as a toddler. God not only showed His healing power by healing Sidney's heart, but He also united a church in a way rarely seen. To this day, our friends tell me that God used their answered prayers for Sidney to heal their hearts as well.

* * *

DeAnn Starling is a mom, wife, attorney, and dog mom. She loves to find humor in everyday life. After graduating from Ole Miss and Vanderbilt Law School, she practiced disability law and wrote grants for children with special needs. Follow her at thebestkindofbroken.com.

Questions for Personal Reflection or Group Discussion

DeAnn and her husband were devastated to learn about their daughter Sidney's severe heart condition, but they found hope and comfort through the prayers of their church. As they prepared for Sidney's surgery, God answered their prayers in miraculous ways, from a better diagnosis to a speedy recovery to exact provision for their daughter's medical costs. Through this journey, Sidney's healing not only touched her family but united a community in prayer and faith.

1. How does DeAnn's story encourage you to trust God's healing power, even when facing difficult or overwhelming circumstances?

2. Have you ever experienced a time when your faith community rallied around you in prayer, and how did that impact your situation?
3. How can this story inspire you to pray specifically and believe that God can answer in powerful and unexpected ways?

We pray that DeAnn's story will remind you of God's faithfulness to hear and answer prayers, no matter how daunting the situation may seem. May it inspire you to lean on your faith community in times of need, trusting that God works through the prayers of His people. Let this testimony encourage you to believe in God's ability to bring healing and unity, even through the most difficult trials.

5

MY DIVINE MATCHMAKER

BY GLENNI LORICK

"*F*ather," I cried as I knelt by my dorm room bed in 1978, "please guide me in choosing a husband. Keep me from making a mistake. I will wait on You!" I opened my red-rimmed eyes and sought comfort in His Word for my hurting heart.

Suddenly, He seared the words of Ecclesiastes 4:9 on my heart: "Two are better than one because they have a good reward for their labor."

"Lord," I prayed, "I promise You I will never commit myself to any man until You give Him this verse." I added, "I promise You I'll never say, 'Yes' to a first date with someone who doesn't love you, and I'll never say 'No' to someone who does."

Five years later, I enrolled in the May term at Mid-America Baptist Theological Seminary in Memphis as I took my initial step toward a master's degree in counseling. Brimming with excitement, I sat expectantly in my Christian education class on the first day.

At that moment, *he* walked through the door. *Oh Lord,* no, *You wouldn't dare,* I thought to myself as I saw his disheveled, wind-

CHRISTIAN WRITERS FOR LIFE

blown hair standing straight up. Fortunately, he didn't sit near me.

The professor had us introduce ourselves. I discovered Keith was from Florida, just like I was. After class, he made a beeline for me. There was no escape. Every day for the next two weeks, he waited to sit with me in chapel. Then, like a lost puppy, he waited until I finished my second class to eat lunch with me.

One Tuesday morning, he cornered me on the sidewalk. "Would you like to go to the zoo with me on Saturday?" he asked hopefully.

Remembering my promise to the Lord, I knew I only had one response: "Sure, that would be fine." I spent the week dreading our date. Finally, on Friday I prayed, "Lord, please help me have a good attitude. After all, it's only one date; I'm not going to marry this guy!"

To my tremendous surprise, our date was terrific. I saw his deep love for Jesus and was drawn to his sense of humor. It ended all too soon, but we both knew we wanted to see more of each other. The next two weeks passed in a flurry of sweet notes on my desk, paper airplanes sent my way in the library, lunch and dinner dates, and growing affection.

That Friday night he took me to Victoria's Station for dinner. At the end of the evening, he kissed me for the first time. Two days later he told me he loved me. "My mind and my will say that, but I just don't feel that way," I responded tentatively.

"Don't worry," he said confidently. "Give it time. I know you will."

I prayed fervently that night. The Lord showed me that I needed to put Keith before the other two suitors in my life. I obeyed, and God instantaneously filled my heart with overwhelming love for him.

The next night I told him, "I want to tell you I love you, but I can't."

"Why not?"

"Because there's a verse God gave me ..."

"Is it in the Old Testament?" he asked. "Is it Ecclesiastes 4:9?" My jaw dropped. Unbeknownst to me, his prayer partner had just prayed that verse with him that morning. God had miraculously answered my prayer.

This year, we celebrate forty years of marriage and ministry together. God blessed us with four children and five grandchildren. I love Keith more now than I ever dreamed possible. My divine matchmaker knew just who I needed!

* * *

Glenni Lorick is a lactation consultant and pastor's wife in Alabama. She and her husband of forty years, Keith, share four children and five grandchildren. Glenni wrote *Fed by Design,* a faith-based, evidence-based how-to manual for breastfeeding mothers. Contact her at www.glennilorick.com or "His by Design with Glenni" on Facebook.

Questions for Personal Reflection or Group Discussion

Glenni trusted God to guide her in choosing a husband, making a promise to wait for His confirmation through Ecclesiastes 4:9. Though initially reluctant, she opened her heart to Keith, and through God's miraculous answer, she knew Keith was the one. Their love story, grounded in faith and prayer, blossomed into a marriage of over forty years, full of blessings.

1. How can Glenni's story encourage you to trust God with your important life decisions, including relationships?
2. Have you ever asked God for specific confirmation in prayer, and how did He answer?

3. How does this story inspire you to wait on God's timing and trust that He knows what's best for you?

We pray that Glenni's story will remind you of the importance of trusting God in your relationships and life decisions. May it inspire you to wait on God's perfect timing, knowing that He is your divine matchmaker who sees the bigger picture. Let this testimony encourage you to bring your desires to Him in prayer, trusting that He will guide you to what is best for your life.

6

THE HIGHWAY OF PRAYER

BY BILL W. KING

We thought that Saturday evening might never arrive. All the plans had been completed and everything was in place. Our morning prayer was mostly one of thanksgiving, but also for our youth to be moved spiritually that evening. Had we truly known what was about to happen, we would have prayed for divine intervention. Before the day ended, I would beg God for a miracle.

I was serving in my first full-time pastorate after seminary. Our church was too small to afford more than one staff member, so I served as pastor and youth minister. Some of our youth had siblings the same age as me. My wife and I had sufficient energy to stay one step ahead, yet enough spiritual development to help with their Christian growth.

A family in our church owned a beautiful farm on Lookout Mountain, not many miles from our church in the valley below. They had invited us to bring the youth up for a cookout and bonfire worship service. We decided to incorporate a hayride to and from the farm. With a trailer full of hay and youth, a truck bed full of chaperones, and an experienced driver pulling us, we hit the road.

21

I had invited two ministerial students from Samford University to come lead us. I brought my guitar and we tried to sing three or four worship songs, right after we had gulped down three or four hotdogs and a few roasted marshmallows. The food was great, but the singing, not so much! After a short devotional message by one of the Samford students, we warmed up with hot chocolate before we loaded up the trailer to head back.

Our route to and from the farm included dirt roads and back streets, except for a half mile stretch on US Highway 11 north of Fort Payne. As we picked up a little speed on the major highway, the cool autumn breeze in our faces refreshed us. Suddenly, Jean shot to her feet and hollered, "He's going to hit us!"

Before I could focus my eyes on the speeding car approaching from behind, I heard the sickening sound of screeching metal and screaming. In horror, I watched as Jean flew out the back of the truck. She fell between the truck and the trailer. I ran to the back of the trailer.

As I rounded the corner, I saw her feet sticking out from underneath. One of our chaperones, a nurse, crawled under the trailer and brought back the unbelievable news that Jean had no pulse. I fell down in the middle of the road. Staring at the two yellow lines, I begged God to let her live. When the firemen jacked up the trailer, her scream was beautiful music to my ears.

The emergency room doctor told me her chest had been crushed. He said, "We need to do surgery now in order to stop the bleeding and save her life."

In the wee hours of the morning, after over three hours of surgery that felt like three days, the surgeon finally emerged. Jean had numerous broken bones and cuts, a punctured and collapsed lung, and a ruptured spleen, diaphragm, and liver. He said, "If she makes it through the night, we may have a chance."

The waiting room had filled up with our family, church members, and friends. The room became one huge prayer closet. Miraculously, no one died that night. Cards, calls, and letters poured in from across the nation from people praying for us. Ten days later, Jean came home from the hospital. Forty-two years later, she is a living testament to answered prayers!

* * *

Bill W. King is a retired pastor and associational missions' strategist. He performs humor through stories and songs as Bro. Billy Bob Bohannon (www.brobillybob.com). He is the author of ten books and writes a weekly syndicated column. He currently serves as bi-vocational pastor of Lanier Baptist Church in Lanett, Alabama.

Questions for Personal Reflection or Group Discussion

Bill experienced a horrifying accident during a youth trip, where his young wife, Jean, was severely injured after being thrown from the back of a truck. In a moment of desperation, Bill cried out to God for her life, and his prayers, along with those of many others, were answered. Despite her extensive injuries, Jean survived, becoming a living testimony to the power of prayer and God's intervention.

1. Have you ever faced a situation where you had to cry out to God for a miracle? How did He respond?
2. How does Bill's story encourage you to trust in God's power to heal and protect, even in life-threatening situations?
3. What role does prayer play in your response to emergencies or crises, and how can this story inspire you to turn to God in faith?

We pray that Bill's story will remind you of the power of prayer in even the most desperate circumstances. May it inspire you to trust in God's ability to work miracles and to intervene when we seek Him in faith. Let this testimony encourage you to rely on prayer, knowing that God hears and answers in ways that can transform even the darkest of moments into stories of hope and healing.

7

U-TURN

BY DONNA SWANN

*T*imes were tough. My husband and I had three children under the age of five. I was a stay-at-home mom, and we owned a business. The business was struggling, we had little money, and our vehicles had issues.

My parents lived two hours away, and it had been a while since I had seen them. When I presented the idea of the children and me going to visit them, my husband wasn't thrilled. "We don't have money and the car isn't reliable." But after a little persuading, he gave in.

We were tooling down the highway, listening to the Barney (the dinosaur) soundtrack. I smelled something and noticed the temperature gauge was on the H. Then, I saw smoke.

I pulled into a gas station parking lot that sat up on a hill. It was a scorching July day. I pulled close to the building so my children would not get hot. The overhang provided shade.

After giving the children reassuring words and a fake smile, I got out and popped the hood. My daddy was a mechanic, so I knew a little bit about cars. I checked the oil and found the dipstick practically blank. I surmised that the car had an oil leak.

I had no money. *My mother told me never to travel without cash*, I thought. I was worried my husband would say, "I knew this wasn't a good idea." *He is going to be upset if he has to leave work to come get me.*

Closing my eyes, I prayed. *Dear Lord, help me. I am stuck with three kids. I have no money. I really want to see Mama. I don't know what to do.*

At the point of tears, I stopped looking under the hood and turned toward the road, standing and staring and at a loss. The highway below was a four-lane road. I noticed a small, worn-out, burgundy truck. It stood out to me because it was in rough condition. It slowed down, made a U-turn, and headed up the hill.

The truck pulled up next to me, and an older gentleman got out. "I noticed you were having some troubles," he said, smiling.

How in the world did he even see me? I am up on the hill, pulled to the side of the building. "Yes, sir. I think I have an oil leak."

He asked how far I had left to go and said, "Well, if we put two quarts of oil in, even with a leak, you'll make it."

I have no money.

He walked into the store and came out with oil. After he put it in and closed the hood, I got out my checkbook. "I don't have any cash, so I'm going to write you a check." *I hope it doesn't bounce.*

"No ma'am. God has blessed me recently with extra. My gift to you."

"You are an answered prayer," I replied.

The gentleman held out both his arms, palms facing up. I looked down and saw scars on both wrists. I know my eyes were huge. *No way, that looks like …*

"I had carpal tunnel surgery recently, and I haven't been able to do a lot. It feels good to get out and help."

"Thank you," was all I could manage to say.

He grinned, waved at the children, got in his beat-up truck, and drove away.

I got in the car and just sat for a second. "Mama, was that man an angel?" my oldest child asked.

"Ya' know what, Emily, I think it just might have been."

* * *

Donna Swann lives in Rome, Georgia. She attends Grace Faith Bible church where her husband, Jack, is the pastor. She has been published in *Good News Magazine* and several Christian anthologies. Smorgasbord of Sisterhood (smorgasbordofsisterhood.com) is a Christian business she shares with her cousin. They spread faith, family and laughter.

Questions for Personal Reflection or Group Discussion

Donna's story recounts a challenging moment on the road when her car overheats, leaving her stranded with three young children. In a time of desperation, she prays for help, and an unexpected stranger answers her prayer by providing the oil needed to get her back on the road. The story reflects the power of prayer and divine intervention, and it leaves Donna wondering if the stranger was an angel sent by God to help her in her time of need.

1. How does Donna's story inspire you to trust in God's provision, even in moments of desperation or uncertainty?
2. Have you ever experienced a situation where you received help in an unexpected way after praying? How did it affect your faith?
3. Donna's child asks if the stranger could have been an angel. Have you ever encountered an angel?

CHRISTIAN WRITERS FOR LIFE

We pray that Donna's story encourages you to pray with faith, knowing that God hears and responds, often in ways that surprise and comfort us. Even in the most difficult moments, His provision can come through unexpected people and circumstances.

8

WHEN WE PRAY IN FAITH

BY ROBIN GRAY

"But he must ask in faith without any doubting ..."
James 1:6a

J sat in my chair, unsure what to do. There were too many bills demanding to be paid and not nearly enough money with just my income. Anxiety pressed in on me from every side. How would I make sure we kept the house? Could I keep the lights on? Would we have food to eat? Up to this point, I'd always counted on my husband to provide and manage finances. In this season of life, I was on my own.

In desperation I cried out to God. *Lord, I don't know how I'll find the money to pay the mortgage, but I have to trust that You are with me in this season. I know You know the answer, and I believe You will provide everything we need.*

In my mind, I knew only God could provide for us while my husband was away. I had no one else to lean on, and I could only work so much while juggling doctors' appointments for our middle daughter.

Just weeks before, I'd shared with my husband a need our girls had for new sports equipment after they made their school teams.

Knowing he could do nothing to help, I'd suggested we both just pray, and I'd ask for help from friends at church.

When those friends didn't come to church that Sunday, I was crushed until I found the envelope tucked in my church bag. It read, "For gloves and spikes." Inside was exactly what their equipment would cost, so I'd already seen God provide for such a frivolous need. Surely, then, He cared enough about our greater physical needs.

Thank You for Your provision. No matter the outcome. I trust that You will provide what we need.

A knock on the door startled me, and I hurriedly finished my prayer as I rose to answer it.

Confusion must have shown on my face because I received an amused smile from the person standing there. She handed me a thick envelope.

"Just wanted you to know we are thinking of you all right now and praying for the family."

I tried to act casual until I could step back inside. The envelope was heavy in my hand, and I escaped to the privacy of my bedroom before opening it. Crisp one-hundred-dollar bills filled the card inside. I slowly counted them out, tears burning my eyes and disbelief filling me as I counted out a full month's mortgage payment.

I fell to my knees as the emotion of that moment overcame me.

"Thank you, God. Thank you, God," I whispered over and over through my tears. "My Provider. Thank you."

As we walked through that challenging season, the provisions for my family came through a variety of God's people. Even before I prayed, God was placing our needs on people's hearts. My earnest prayers for provision and comfort were all met in His divine time, often before I expected them.

When we faithfully ask God to provide, He will with abundance.

* * *

Robin Gray lives in Virginia with her childhood sweetheart-turned-husband, four adult children, and three dogs. She has served alongside her husband in various ministry roles, although they feel a special call to underserved communities. Together, they share God's Word through their online ministry, InTheGrayArea.com.

Questions for Personal Reflection or Group Discussion

Robin's story reflects the power of praying in faith, even when facing overwhelming financial and personal challenges. In a season of uncertainty, Robin placed her trust in God's provision, and He answered her prayers in ways that surpassed her expectations. Through the generosity of others, God met her needs before she even realized it.

1. How does Robin's faith in God's provision encourage you to trust Him more in times of financial or emotional difficulty?
2. Have there been times in your life when you prayed in faith and God provided in unexpected or miraculous ways?
3. What can you learn from Robin's unwavering trust in God's ability to meet her needs, even when the outcome seemed uncertain?

We pray that Robin's story reminds you that God hears and answers prayers when we ask in faith. Just as He provided for Robin and her family, He is able to meet your needs, often in ways beyond what you expect. May this story encourage you to bring your requests to God, trusting Him to provide in His perfect timing.

9

A SIMPLE "YES" WILL SUFFICE

BY EDWARD BEAM

*H*as God ever verbally spoken to you? I have had several running conversations, the first of which I will share with you.

I had taken two from my youth group to a Promise Keepers conference. For those of you unfamiliar with that ministry, back in the nineties, stadiums full of men were challenged to lead God-centered lives. I was driving back with the two of them asleep in the back seat, and I heard a simple message directly from God Himself: *You must pray.*

Of course I wanted to know why, but all I got was that something life-changing was going to happen to one of these two. The second thing was that I must be ready to up my game and be ready to step into the fire. I didn't understand this part of the message, but prayer is one thing I could do, so I did pray for these two young men and thought nothing of it.

That was Saturday night. The next night, my phone rang at 11:00 PM, which was not uncommon. It was one of these young men, and he wanted me to come over. I was used to such requests. His home was the gathering point for our youth group at all hours of the day or night. This night was different.

While we were at the conference, his mother left her house and marriage for another man. She left her family, and for a teenager, this was a major trauma that he could not grasp. What I didn't know at the time was that I was the last one on his phone list that night, and had I not responded, he probably would not be here today.

Unfortunately (or fortunately), I didn't have any of the answers he wanted that night. What God did show me that night was a strategy that quite honestly changed both of our lives. What I did know is that we needed to surround the young man with love.

Two days later, we as a group wrapped our arms around him and began an adventure together. The entire summer involved supporting and encouraging him in every way possible. Several nights a week were spent in his house just hanging out. Preaching wasn't necessary. What was necessary was being the hands and feet of Jesus.

It's been more than twenty-five years since I had my first running conversation with God. Both of our lives changed that fateful night. I am proud to say that we are not only survivors, but our faith went to a new level. We are still good friends and just saw each other again for the first time in many years. To have him say that I was one of the most positive people he's ever met brought me to tears.

Has God spoken like that to you or challenged you to pray? If He does, He will probably want you to do something, so be open to that. He challenged me to pray that night. There is no telling what would have happened had I not done that.

He's told me to pray on other occasions. One time I actually prayed for a change in the weather, and you know what? It happened. It was the strangest and neatest thing to see the stars and moon appear simply because you asked them to.

Be open to God's challenges to pray. Be ready. A simple "yes" will suffice to begin a whole new and exciting chapter in your life.

* * *

Edward Beam's most recent book, *The Gospel of I AM*, was published on Amazon. This book is a letter written by Jesus Christ to the people of today. Above all, this book brings a message of hope. The book's website, www.thegospelofiam.com, provides more information about the book and a roadmap for transformation.

Questions for Personal Reflection or Group Discussion

Edward experienced a direct conversation with God, calling him to pray for one of the young men in his youth group. Though he didn't fully understand why at the time, his obedience to God's voice led to him being present when that young man faced a life-changing trauma. By simply saying "yes" to God, Edward became an instrument of love and support, forever impacting the life of this teenager and deepening his own faith in the process.

1. Have you ever felt God calling you to pray for someone? How did you respond, and what happened as a result?
2. How does Edward's story encourage you to be open to God's voice, even when you don't fully understand the situation?
3. What steps can you take to be more attuned to God's call, and how can you be ready to respond with a simple "yes"?

We pray that Edward's story will remind you that God often speaks to us in simple yet powerful ways, and a willingness to obey can have life-changing effects. May it inspire you to be open to God's call to pray for others, knowing that your obedience can be the first step in a remarkable journey of faith. Let this testimony encourage you to listen closely for God's voice, trusting that He will guide you into opportunities to be His hands and feet in the lives of others.

10

I KNEW RAIN WAS COMING

BY CHERYL GORE POLLARD

"Whoever humbles himself like a child is the greatest in the
Kingdom of Heaven."
Matthew 18:3

*T*he end of July is always hot, humid, and sticky in West
Georgia. It was the same in 1977. There I was, a tired
single mom struggling to pay bills and feed two children,
preparing to preserve tomatoes for our depleted pantry. One
thing I'd learned is that God provides. He doesn't always hand
provisions out on a silver platter, but if we're willing to do our
part, we're extra blessed—sometimes through everyday tasks.

We'd spent that morning at my parents', filling two big buckets
with tomatoes. Daddy always had an unbelievable garden and
shared it with everyone. Today, I was the happy recipient.

We lugged the heavy buckets home—an older, non-air-
conditioned mobile home sitting right under the sun. Summers
were hot in there, even at night.

I began heating water and jars, praying everything went
smoothly. Even without the extra heat and steam needed to

blanch tomatoes, it was nothing less than a baking oven inside. It was unbearable, so we moved our "canning area" outside.

We situated large dishpans and dragged the water hose close to cool hot tomatoes. It was miserably hot. The air was still, humid, and oppressively heavy.

I felt ashamed having to recruit my children to help. But there wasn't one complaining word from them. My heart ached seeing their red, hot faces, knowing they'd rather be someplace else. Somewhere cool.

When the water was hot enough, I carefully carried it outside and poured it over the tomatoes. We sat on overturned buckets and doorsteps, waiting for the tomato skins to start splitting for easy peeling. We had no porch or covering, so there we sat, hot and sticky, while tiny rivulets of sweat ran down our faces and dripped off our chins. It almost tickled as it ran down our backs, plastering cloth to skin. Sonny and Ginger were so patient, wiping sweat and hoping for a quick finishing up. I promised to take them to the creek for a cooling swim later. They perked up a bit. *Thank you, God!*

Ginger pointed to the buckets. "Tomato skins splitting!"

"Ginger," I said. "Get the hose ready."

Sonny jumped up and ran inside. I was too busy to pay much attention.

I carefully poured scalding water from buckets onto the ground while Ginger directed cool water over the tomatoes. Just then Sonny came back, hopping lightly from the door to the ground. Suddenly, a little breeze stirred. He picked up a tomato and began to peel. The breeze grew stronger.

The sky darkened, and chest-hammering thunder shook the air. We realized we were in for a sudden summer storm. Grabbing buckets and dishpans, we rushed inside. The wind flowed through open windows and doors, chasing heat away. Then the bottom fell out. Such a refreshing blessing.

"I can't believe our luck," Ginger laughed. "Thank you, God, for the cooling rain."

Sonny looked up, a happy gap-toothed grin on his face. "I knew it was coming," he said confidently.

"So, you can tell the future?" I asked.

"What do you think I did when I ran inside? I got down beside my bed and prayed for rain so we wouldn't be outside in the heat." He dipped his head. "I knew rain was coming. I asked God for it."

My heart burst with joy at this revelation. If we pray as a child with unfaltering, endless trust, and faith that God will answer our prayers, He will. *God answers prayers.*

That is exactly what happens when we pray.

* * *

Cheryl Gore Pollard is a mother and grandmother living in rural West Georgia. She is active in church and community activities, a retired teacher who keeps busy sharing time with her family, writing, gardening, and painting. She is the author of seven books and several short stories.

Questions for Personal Reflection or Group Discussion

Cheryl shares a beautiful story about her family's experience canning tomatoes on a sweltering summer day in Georgia. Despite the heat, her son, Sonny, prayed for rain with unwavering faith, and God answered his prayer, bringing cool relief just when they needed it most. The story illustrates the power of childlike faith and the importance of trusting God to answer prayers in His perfect timing.

1. How does Sonny's faith in God's ability to send rain inspire you to pray with more trust and confidence?

2. Have there been times in your life when you prayed for something and God answered in a way that felt like a direct blessing, just as the rain was for Cheryl and her children?

3. What can you learn from the way Sonny prayed with simple, unshakable belief that God would provide exactly what they needed?

We pray that Cheryl's story will remind you to pray with childlike faith, trusting that God hears your prayers and responds with love and provision. Whether big or small, your requests are important to God, and His answers often come in ways that refresh and renew us just when we need them most.

11

AGAINST ALL ODDS

BY KAREN O. ALLEN

"*Y*ou *will* be a mother."

The words stumbled out of my mouth. The conversation had taken an unexpected turn. Mandy called to ask a few questions about her mom's cancer diagnosis after hearing me speak about my book *Confronting Cancer with Faith*. I knew Mandy's name from the prayer list. She was dealing with a serious vascular issue. Her name was well known at church, but no one knew the gut-wrenching, soul-searching ache in her heart.

Like Hannah, Mandy desperately longed to be a mother. The gaping void in her heart was as big as a seedless avocado. She endured not one but two pregnancies, which both ended in miscarriages. Doctors said her autoimmune disorder prevented a full-term pregnancy. They were right.

Mandy and I became fast friends, meeting and swapping stories.

"I want to show you something," Mandy said. The photo album was neatly arranged. As I flipped the pages, the sting of tears filled my eyes. I could not help but gaze upon the ultrasound scans of unborn lives that never saw the outside of their mother's womb.

Weeks later, I received a call. "Guess what, guess what? I'm pregnant!" The speck of life growing inside Mandy appeared to be the answer to our prayers.

She provided periodic updates, thanking me for my prayers and encouragement. Every day drew closer to the much-anticipated due date.

Then, one evening, Mandy called. Her voice was soft and weighted. "I lost the baby."

A third miscarriage. I was living this pregnancy with her; now I mourned with her. How could this happen? This was supposed to be the one to make it full-term—the one that Mandy would finally hold in her arms.

"Thank you for allowing me to fall in love again," she said as I cringed.

"You *will* be a mother," I said again, offering no explanation. My unwavering words had a tone of authority. Deep in my gut, I believed them.

Mandy and Craig reinstated the steps they started earlier for adoption. Progression was painstakingly slow and expensive. Finally, it was time for a home visit. Then devastating news came.

Mandy had breast cancer.

Adoption was out of the question; her options were exhausted. Once again, my faith rose to a surprising level of conviction. I spent abandoned time in prayer, pleading on behalf of my friend.

Please, Lord, please allow Mandy and Craig to be parents somehow, some way.

As if circumstances could not be any more difficult, Mandy's job as a labor and delivery nurse was exceedingly challenging. The Scripture "All things are possible with God" popped into my head. The words were empowering as I proclaimed them aloud to Mandy.

Adoption efforts were withdrawn, giving priority to Mandy's

health. She underwent a mastectomy with reconstruction in the hospital where she worked.

Two days after surgery, I got a call at work. "Pray, pray, pray," Craig exclaimed. "There may be an opportunity."

A single young woman in labor arrived at the emergency room. "Does anyone want this baby?" she wryly inquired.

Mandy's coworker spoke up. "I know someone."

Could this be happening? Could this be the miracle, the impossible thing we'd been waiting for? Yes, oh yes, it was. What an incredible, remarkable, astonishing, unmistakable answer to prayer!

I visited Mandy, Craig, and Michael the next day in the hospital. Soon after, I attended Michael's adoption at the courthouse. Birthday parties and Christmases have come and gone as I have watched Michael grow into a handsome young man. He looks nothing like his parents, but maybe miracle babies aren't supposed to.

* * *

Retired from cancer research in Birmingham, Alabama, **Karen O. Allen** fills her days writing, traveling, walking dogs, and playing the organ. Her unique devotional and coloring book, *Outta My Mind, Into His Heart,* brings hope to the mental health community. Join Karen's bi-weekly Ewe R Blessed blog (http://ewerblessed.com) for uplifting stories.

Questions for Personal Reflection or Group Discussion

Karen witnessed Mandy's heartbreaking journey through multiple miscarriages and a cancer diagnosis, but she continued to pray with faith, believing that Mandy would one day become a mother. Against all odds, God answered those prayers in a miraculous way through adoption. Mandy and her husband were blessed with a son, Michael, in the most unexpected of circumstances.

1. How does Mandy's story encourage you to trust in God's timing, even when hope seems lost?
2. Have you ever experienced or witnessed a situation where God provided in an unexpected and miraculous way?
3. How does this story inspire you to continue praying and believing in God's promises, even when the road ahead seems difficult?

We pray that Mandy's story will remind you of God's power to work miracles, even in the face of impossible odds. May it encourage you to keep faith in God's promises, trusting that He has a plan for your life that may unfold in surprising ways. Let this testimony inspire you to persist in prayer and believe that with God, all things are possible, no matter the challenges you face.

12

MORE THAN EXPECTED

BY MISHAEL AUSTIN WITTY

*L*ord, can you please send us one thousand dollars? It was an audacious request, but not out of bounds. A few months before, I had asked God for the same amount, and He'd supplied it within the week.

Now, our bills piled up and spilled into overdue territory like an overwatered plant. I bit my lip and exhaled as I waited. *What about five hundred dollars?* The answer thumped against my chest wall, stealing a breath.

My racing heart thudded inside my breastbone. I tapped my fingers over it in a mimicking pattern. *Okay. Five hundred.* Why argue with God?

As the days passed without the promised money materializing, seeds of doubt and disappointment littered my mind like the maple helicopters falling to the green grass outside my window.

"Here, Mommy. I made this for you." My older daughter's words drew my attention away from my dark thoughts. She handed me a picture she'd drawn on a sheet of copy paper. "Can I have more? I ran out."

Blinking back tears, I smiled into her hope-filled eyes. "We'll see what we can do about that." *God, can we please have some drawing paper, in addition to the five hundred dollars?*

Hours later, I received an email from a friend.

How are you? Do you need anything?

My finger dragged the mouse over to the Reply button, but I hesitated. Should I reveal our financial struggles or keep that between me and God?

His still, small voice whispered, *Tell her everything.*

I gritted my teeth and pounded out a message, telling her about asking God for five hundred dollars. I left out the part about the copy paper.

She responded with, *I think I can give you what God said to expect.*

My hands collapsed against the keyboard and the words on the screen blurred in a teary haze. I thanked her and God and arranged for her to meet with my husband later in the week since he worked near her home. The cloud of sadness evaporated. One half of my prayer had been answered.

On the appointed day, my husband came back home carrying a wad of cash and two bulging red plastic bags.

I took them from him. "What are these? Where did they come from?"

He rubbed a hand against the back of his neck. "Mary gave them to me with the money. Something told her she needed to stop by Staples and pick up two packs of copy paper to give to us too. She didn't understand why, but she had to do it."

I stacked the paper on the floor between us. Seconds later, I was on my knees, shaking with laughter.

My husband raised an eyebrow and stepped closer. "What's so funny?"

Slapping the palm of my hand on top of the stack, I took in a calming, cleansing breath. "I asked God for one thousand dollars. He didn't give us that, but He sent us one thousand sheets of copy paper. I didn't know how we were going to get more paper, but God did."

My older daughter walked into the room. She hugged her father and pointed to the packages of paper on the floor. "Is that my paper?"

I nodded and smoothed her hair back over her shoulder. "Yes. It's a gift from a friend and our Heavenly Father. And it's all yours. God answered both of our prayers."

* * *

Mishael Austin Witty is a wife, mother, and nature lover who writes about the things she's most passionate about—that includes faith, family, food, and fitness. You can find more of her faith-centered writing over at Patheos: https://www.patheos.-com/blogs/doyouwanttogetwell/mishael-austin-witty/. Check out her self-published fiction and nonfiction on Amazon: https://www.amazon.com/stores/Mishael-Austin-Witty/author/B007R5PTO8.

Questions for Personal Reflection or Group Discussion

Mishael found herself with mounting unpaid bills and, in a moment of honesty, asked God for financial help. Although the money didn't arrive right away, God answered the prayer in a way she didn't expect—providing not only money, but also the drawing paper her daughter had asked for. Mishael was reminded that God's provision may look different than what we anticipate, but it always meets our needs perfectly.

1. How does Mishael's story encourage you to trust God's provision, even when the answer doesn't come in the way you expect?

2. Have you ever experienced a time when God answered a prayer in an unexpected or even humorous way?
3. How can this story inspire you to trust that God knows your needs and will provide for them, even down to the smallest details?

We pray that Mishael's story will remind you of God's loving attention to the details of your life, and His ability to meet both big and small needs in ways you may not expect. May it encourage you to keep trusting in His provision, knowing that He hears every prayer. Let this testimony inspire you to ask boldly, trust deeply, and find joy in how God answers your prayers in His perfect timing and manner.

13

WHEN GOD SENT A PASTOR

BY KATHY BLEY

Bam! Thump, thump, thump. Our tire blew. My husband and I were on a part of the interstate with no development nearby. It was late Sunday afternoon in September 1983. Earlier that day, we were happily out looking for a house to buy and had found the perfect lot where we hoped to build our dream home. Our spirits were definitely dampened by this unexpected turn of events.

Anxiety filled my heart since we were on the shoulder of a busy road, but I trusted the abilities of my husband to take care of the situation. He went to the trunk of our white Mazda 626 to get the spare. Moments later, he came to my passenger side window and told me not to worry, but that that the spare was flat also. Definitely an unforeseen problem! This was pre-cell phone, so we could not just call someone to help. My heart was pounding as we prayed, but we knew that God hears our prayers.

Shortly after moving to Birmingham, we needed a new washer and dryer. We had three hundred dollars that we could spend. In 1982, the best place to find used items for sale was the bulletin board at the local grocery store. We went to our nearby Western supermarket to see what we could find. A washer and dryer were

49

listed. We tore off the tab with the phone number and went home to make the phone call. Yes, they still had the set and the price was, miraculously, exactly three hundred dollars!

On a hot and muggy morning the previous summer, I went for a run. After the run, I felt really bad—very dizzy, maybe a little dehydrated. When I got to the door, I realized I was locked out of our townhouse. The key was still hanging on the hook inside, and my husband was out of town.

Most of the neighbors had gone to work, leaving few cars in the parking area around me. I lay on my driveway, praying for someone to help me. I heard the sound of a door closing about eight townhouses down. A neighbor who I didn't know was coming out of her house. I moved as fast as I could muster and made my way to her. She took one look at me and realized I needed help. After getting me some water and letting me cool off inside, she drove me fifteen minutes to the rental office to get another key. What a blessing she was that day!

Back on that hot September afternoon, we got out of the car and stuck our thumbs out, hoping someone would stop to help. Hitchhiking wasn't as unusual in the 1980s. My fear levels rose with every car that drove by us without stopping.

We decided to stop and pray, asking God to please send someone to help us. Desperation was creeping in to my mind. A green car with a man in it drove by us and then came to a stop a short distance past. He slowly backed up on the shoulder.

We got in and thanked him over and over for stopping. He said that he was a pastor heading home to Pensacola, and that he never stopped for hitchhikers. However, that day, he felt God tell him to pull over and give us a helping hand. He drove us to a gas station where we filled the spare with air and then back to our car on the interstate. God heard our prayers and sent the help we needed!

* * *

Kathy Bley lives in Alabama and has four books available on Amazon: *Dare to Be Healthy Now: A Scripture-based Wellness Journal, Standing in the Gap for Our Kids,* and her latest release, *Standing in the Gap for Our Grandkids.* Three grandkids call her Noni!

Questions for Personal Reflection or Group Discussion

Kathy's story of an unexpected tire blowout and the miraculous provision of a pastor to help them reflects the beauty of God's timely intervention. Through prayer and trust, Kathy and her husband experienced God's care, even in the midst of a difficult situation, when a pastor who normally didn't stop for hitchhikers obeyed God's prompting to help.

1. How does this story inspire you to trust God to send help in difficult situations, even when circumstances seem hopeless?
2. Have you experienced a moment when God sent someone unexpectedly to help you in a time of need? How did this impact your faith?
3. What can you learn from Kathy's response of prayer and trust when they faced an unexpected challenge? How can you apply that to challenges you may face today?

We pray that Kathy's story encourages you to trust that God hears and answers your prayers, even when you face unforeseen difficulties. He is faithful to provide help, often in ways we don't expect, and He uses others to be His hands and feet. May this story remind you to trust in God's perfect timing and provision.

14

MIRACLE AT MARSH HARBOUR

BY ESTHER BANDY

*A*s we sailed to the Bahamas, the salty breeze blew our son's blonde hair, and his hazel eyes sparkled. Billy waved to seagulls swooping in the air, laughed at dolphins jumping through waves, and entertained his grandparents.

My dad anchored his forty-four-foot sailboat in Marsh Harbour, then we all rode to the dock in Dad's small powerboat. We enjoyed conch fritters at dinner before strolling around the island. Later that night, we talked and gazed at glistening stars while the sailboat rocked gently.

In the morning, my husband and I rode in Dad's little rubber dinghy to the island. It was our first ministry trip, and we asked the Lord to guide us as we explored the island and offered gospel tracts to the people we met. The following day, we took our cardboard puppet stage and puppets in the dinghy to the island. Wind gusts blew against the sail-like stage, and we almost capsized.

Lord, please help us!

We reached the dock safely and set up the puppet stage. Then, I climbed in with our puppets while Jim interacted with the gathering crowd. When Jim knocked on the cardboard box, the puppets appeared. Jim shared the gospel with the puppets, then he talked with the crowd while I climbed out of the box and handed out tracts.

A man introduced himself. "I saw you in your little rubber dinghy, and you almost capsized. Will you do more puppet shows?"

Jim nodded. "We plan to."

The man pointed nearby. "I'm pastor of that church. If you want, you can store your stage there until you need it."

The next day, the Lord led us down a narrow path to a wooden shack. The door was like a magnet pulling us closer, but a growling dog bared its teeth and blocked our way.

"Lord, is this where you want us? Please help us."

God's presence overwhelmed me. When we stepped forward, the dog backed away.

Jim knocked, but nobody answered. He knocked again, but still no answer. We prayed again, then an angry-looking man opened the door, glaring at us.

Jim introduced himself and said, "God wants you to know that He loves you."

The old man shook his head and whispered. "Nobody loves me."

Jim leaned forward. "God does."

We talked a long time, then the man finally invited us inside. We saw a rope tied to the rafter, and the old man admitted that he'd planned to kill himself. After we shared the gospel and answered his questions, he trusted in Christ. Before we left him that day, he promised not to harm himself. We later introduced him to the pastor we'd met.

Months later, we got a letter from the old man. He'd been attending the pastor's church and was making new friends. Life was worth living after all. Two years after that, we moved to Mexico as faith missionaries. We didn't know what to expect, but we knew we could ask the Lord to guide us, and He would.

"I will instruct thee and teach thee in the way which thou shalt go:
I will guide thee with mine eye."
Psalm 32:8

"Trust in the Lord with all thine heart; and lean not unto thine
own understanding. In all thy ways acknowledge him, and he shall
direct thy paths."
Proverbs 3:5-6

"Fear thou not; for I am with thee: be not dismayed; for I am thy
God: I will strengthen thee; yea, I will help thee; yea, I will uphold
thee with the right hand of my righteousness."
Isaiah 41:10

* * *

When **Esther Bandy** was five, she heard the gospel in a Good
News Club and received Christ. She's worked as a nurse, a
missionary, a Child Evangelism Fellowship director, and a
Spanish teacher. Her novel, *Under the Tangerine Tree*, was
published in 2022. She's also been published in four anthologies.

Questions for Personal Reflection or Group Discussion

Esther shares her powerful story of God's protection and
guidance during a ministry trip to the Bahamas. Despite facing
challenges like strong winds and a dangerous encounter with a
man on the brink of ending his life, Esther and her husband
followed God's leading. Through their faith and persistence, they
were able to share the gospel, save a life, and witness the power of
God's love in action. This story reminds us that when we trust in
God's guidance, even in the face of obstacles, He can work
miracles.

1. How does Esther's experience of trusting in God's guidance during difficult circumstances encourage you to seek His direction in your own life?
2. Have you ever faced a situation where you felt uncertain or in danger but later saw how God's presence protected and guided you?
3. What can you learn from Esther and Jim's perseverance and faith as they continued their ministry, even when faced with opposition and potential danger?

We pray that Esther's story inspires you to trust in God's guidance and protection, no matter the challenges or fears you may face. God's love is powerful, and His guidance is always available when we seek Him with a willing heart.

15

THE ANSWER

BY BETTY BULLARD

I thought this time of deafening quietness after the children were asleep would soon be over. Daytime was lively and full of meeting needs. It was the nights I dreaded.

I was not always husbandless, just many days and many weeks. The house without another adult was lonely, and I could not fill that space. And so, I prayed. Quite selfishly, to be sure. I simply wanted my husband to have a job where he was not away from us so much of the time. I prayed if it could be in God's will, He would send another work opportunity for my husband.

And He did. Four years of *faith growing* and *faith slowing* crept by, but in God's timing, He gave me, as Psalm 37:4 says, "the desires of my heart."

After meeting Ray and Joye Rust, we were elated. There was no doubt—they would be God's best leaders and mentors in this exciting and challenging new work. I believed with all my heart this was God's will for our family.

After difficult, soul-searching days, my husband did not. A telephone call was made. The offer was rejected, and my husband was off to his next assignment.

That night, totally disheartened, I collapsed onto our couch planning to cry and pray. I pictured my husband lying down to sleep, never considering this opportunity again. Seemingly out of nowhere, a prayer came to my mind, and it replayed continually for days: *Dear God, if this work is your will, please let him be miserable and don't let him sleep.*

My husband is always full of optimism, and no matter the concerns of the day, when night comes, he sleeps.

Finally, the evening came for his return. There were the familiar sounds of his car in our driveway, the latching of the car door, the slamming of the trunk, and the crunching roll of the suitcase on the paved path. I stood in our entry hall, dimly lit by a small lamp atop a church's cast-off music chest.

As much as my husband loved his work, he missed us terribly when he was gone. His homecoming was always a celebration, but not that night. His face was drawn and pensive. "I'm afraid I've made a mistake. I've been miserable, and I haven't been able to sleep."

With me trembling and him weary, we sat opposite each other in our softly lit den.

I waited. The story came of sleepless nights and his not wanting to hear of a new leading from God. Giving up his loved work had been too painful. He did not want to make the call to Dr.

Rust for fear of seeming immature and unsure of himself. "I need to wait some days and see if this feeling passes."

It was then my turn to tell my story of the prayer God had put on my heart.

After hearing it, he stood and slowly walked to the telephone on our kitchen wall. His words were measured and deliberate. He was a driven, energetic thirty-four-year-old wanting to appear competent and in control, yet humility was the only road to walk. "Dr. Rust, I may have answered too soon. I may have made a mistake. Have you moved to another candidate?"

I knew by the conversation that Dr. Rust had not. In moments, we were once again sitting opposite each other. My husband looked incredulous as he almost whispered Dr. Rust's response: "No, George, I haven't moved on. I was waiting on your call. Joye told me you would call."

* * *

Betty Bullard is a writer in retirement. She has spent her life working with children and teachers, and teaching women's Bible study classes. She and her husband live in her hometown of Greenville, South Carolina. There she finds joy in her family, friends, church, and writing.

Questions for Personal Reflection or Group Discussion

Betty shares a heartfelt story of longing and prayer as she waited for her husband to find a job that would keep him home more often. Though the opportunity came, her husband initially turned it down, only to realize through sleepless nights that God had other plans. Betty's persistent prayer that he be made "miserable" if it wasn't God's will became the key to opening a path forward for their family.

1. How does Betty's story demonstrate the importance of persistence and patience in prayer?
2. Have you ever prayed for something specific, only to see God answer in a way that you didn't expect? How did you feel when the answer came?
3. What can you learn from the way Betty trusted in God's timing and allowed Him to work in her husband's heart, rather than trying to force the outcome herself?

We pray that Betty's story reminds you that God is always at work, even in moments of uncertainty or waiting. Sometimes His answers come in unexpected ways, but they always align with His perfect will and timing. Let this be an encouragement to trust in God's plan, even when the answer seems delayed or different than anticipated.

16

$15K IN ONE DAY!

BY JESSE NELSON

*G*od did it!! Wow! I can't believe it. He really did it! After four months of prayers, presentations, doubts and fears, I finally received good news.

In September 2011, I was the pastor of New Vision Church, a ministry initiated in my childhood community by several churches in Dothan, Alabama. We had fewer than fifteen members, which included my family of four. We had been meeting for months, but it was difficult getting adults to attend service at 3:00 PM. So we decided to change our focus to children.

With a demand for children's activities in the community, this plan sounded great. But we had two problems. First, we didn't have our own building. Second, we didn't have enough money to buy a building. But we *needed* a building and believed God would provide. So we decided to walk by faith and not our bank account.

One afternoon in January 2012, Dr. Lewis, my support pastor, called me to meet him to see a building. "Wow, this place is perfect," I said. I envisioned the children running and laughing. I knew this was the place God destined for us. However, it was $135,000. I told Dr. Lewis it was too much. He reminded me that nothing was too much for God and said, "Let's pray for it." So every day, Jacey, my four-year-old daughter, and I went by the property to pray. I wanted her to see the power of faith and prayer.

A month later I was notified that the price had dropped from $135,000 to $85,000. It felt like God had just given us $50,000 toward the purchase. I went to meet a realtor.

I told the realtor, "I have no money. I have to go and raise it. So, I will need at least ninety days to close on it." To our surprise, the sellers agreed to our offer of $85,000 and ninety-day closing. Now I had to get the money.

Dr. Lewis had experience in raising money for buildings, so he helped me create my presentation package for fundraising. After meeting with a loan officer and a few churches, I was pre-approved for $65,000 and had $20,000 pledged from my partner churches. I thought I had everything I needed, until…

On closing day, my realtor called with bad news and good news. The bad news was the bank wanted another $15,000 by end of day to close the loan. The good news was my realtor donated his $5,000 commission toward my down payment. So, I only needed $10,000 by 5:00 PM.

It took me ninety days to get $20,000; how could I get $10,000 in a day?

Later that day, I met with my Friday prayer group. We asked God for the $10,000 as confirmation that He wanted us to possess the property.

But five o'clock came, and I didn't have the $10,000. My vision of kids running and laughing in the field was fading away.

Around 10:00 PM, one of my prayer partners called me. He said, "Jesse, you got the $10,000. You got it!!" He told me how two men heard about my dilemma and pledged $5,000 each.

I yelled, "God did it!! Wow! I can't believe it. He really did it! Jacey, come here! Come here! We got the building! We got the building!" Jacey started laughing, dancing, and praising God because God did it! He provided $15k in a day. After making several phone calls, I went to bed with a smile on my face, dreaming about children laughing and playing in the field.

* * *

Jesse Nelson is a pastor, speaker, and writer. He enjoys sharing life with his wife (Catesha) and two children. He pastors Macedonia Baptist Church in Panama City, Florida, and is the mayor of Lynn Haven, Florida. His publications include *My Prayer Book*, *We Survived Hurricane Michael*, and *Preaching Life-Changing Sermons*.

Questions for Personal Reflection or Group Discussion

Jesse was faced with a seemingly impossible financial challenge to purchase a building for his church, but through prayer and faith, he witnessed God's provision. Despite setbacks, he continued to trust God and was amazed when, at the last moment, God provided exactly what was needed. This experience deepened Jesse's faith and served as a powerful testimony of God's ability to answer prayers in unexpected ways.

1. When have you faced a challenge that seemed impossible, and how did you trust God through it?
2. How can you include others, like Jesse did with his daughter, in your faith journey?
3. What does this story teach you about persistence in prayer, even when the outcome seems uncertain?

We pray that Jesse's story will remind you of the power of prayer and God's ability to provide in ways beyond what we can imagine. May this testimony encourage you to trust in God's timing and provision, especially when obstacles seem insurmountable. Let it inspire you to continue in faith, knowing that God is always working for our good, even when the solution seems out of reach.

17

DESPERATE FOR ANSWERS

BY SARA THORNBURGH

*H*ave you ever been so desperate for answers from the Lord that you didn't know what to do? Have you ever asked the Lord to help you find something and the Lord answered you in a dream?

I'll never forget the time I was visiting the family of some friends. We stayed overnight and I slept in the camper where I kept my belongings during our stay.

As our visit came to an end, we gathered our belongings and headed home. At home, I started unpacking and realized something—a very important something—was missing. My phone.

Where could it be? I prayed as I frantically continued digging through my suitcase and other belongings, hoping I'd find it but to no avail.

Hours of searching turned into days of searching, and I was beginning to feel more desperate than ever.

Beyond discouraged and ready for answers, I cried out to the Lord once again in hopes that He would somehow shine a light on the location of my phone.

You're probably thinking, *It's just a phone*, right? That is true, but for me, it was my lifeline to stay in touch with friends, family, and my transportation. I was so desperate for answers.

One night, after I searched and prayed for several days, the Lord gave me a dream. In this dream, the Lord showed me where my phone was. In the dream, I saw my phone under a pillow in the camper. I told my friends, who in turn told their family.

They went to look in the camper, in the area they were told, and at first they couldn't find the missing lifeline. But they kept searching until, inside the pillowcase, they discovered my phone.

Now, while the location of my phone in the dream and in reality weren't perfect matches, I know the dream was still the answer to my prayers. If it had not been for the dream, we would not have known where to look and may never have found my phone.

When you're feeling hopeless, discouraged, or just stuck, pray and cry out to the Lord. Keep pushing and praying until you see a breakthrough. He cares. He's right beside you, lifting you up, carrying you, giving you the strength you need.

He hears your cries and answers them, it may not always look the way we think it should or want it to, just remember to trust Him. He knows what's best for us.

I hope and pray you are truly encouraged by this story.

"Ask, and it will be given to you; Seek, and you will find; Knock, and it will be opened to you."
Matthew 7:7

"Be anxious for nothing, but in everything by prayer and supplication with thanksgiving, let your requests be made known to God. And the peace of God, which surpasses all comprehension, will guard your hearts and your minds in Christ Jesus."
Philippians 4:6-7

* * *

Sara Thornburgh is an emerging writer and author with four other award-winning stories: "Cherished Memories," "Make a Joyful Noise," "Fall Foods," and "Cinnamon and Apples No More." You can find out more about Sara's work at "Sara Thornburgh— Author" on Facebook.

Questions for Personal Reflection or Group Discussion

Sara shares a heartfelt story of how she lost her phone during a visit and felt desperate for answers as she searched for days without success. After praying fervently, she received a dream from the Lord, guiding her to where her phone was located. The dream didn't give an exact match to the phone's location, but it provided the direction needed to eventually find it, demonstrating how God cares about even the small things in our lives and answers prayers in ways we might not expect.

1. How does Sara's story encourage you to trust God even in small, everyday matters? Have you ever experienced a moment where God answered your prayer in an unexpected or miraculous way?
2. In what ways can we apply the lesson of perseverance in prayer, as Sara did, when we feel desperate for answers or guidance?
3. How does this story illustrate the importance of trusting that God cares about our concerns, no matter how big or small they might seem?

We pray that Sara's story encourages you to bring all your concerns—big or small—to God, knowing that He listens and answers in His perfect timing. Let her experience remind you that perseverance in prayer, coupled with trust in God's care, can lead to miraculous breakthroughs when we least expect them.

BEANS, BILLS, AND BLESSINGS

BY CYNTHIA MARTIN

The grocery list mocked me with its meager offerings: beans and rice again. *How can this be?* I thought. My husband, Doug, a financially conservative man, insisted on a tight budget, despite our healthy savings. We had more than enough income coming in. Frustration bubbled up. "Do we have to live like this?"

Doug, engrossed in the news, barely glanced up. "We're saving for the future."

"But the future includes present needs," I pleaded. Feeling helpless, I blurted, "How am I supposed to manage? Do you think I am not going to get an electric bill this month?" It was a desperate question.

My faith journey was new. I was reading the Bible and praying more, not just at meals. I wanted to be a real Christian—I wanted to be totally committed—but was I? Could I trust Him even in these situations?

The next morning, a surprise was in the mail: the electric bill with a credit balance. A system error resulted in a billing error. Relief mixed with wonder—could this be an answer?

Months later, another challenge arose. Our church's annual

camping trip, a cherished tradition, was approaching. "Doug," I said, "we need a camper. The girls and I look forward to going on this trip more than any other thing in the year."

In previous years, my mom had loaned us her camper. A few months prior, though, she had sold it. The resource I had counted previously on was no longer available.

Doug, predictably stoic, shook his head. "I think the girls would rather go to Disney. We don't have room for a camper in the budget."

Disheartened but not defeated, I spent days searching. *Lord, I prayed, show us a way if You will let us to go. Lord, I am trying to honor my husband. I do not see how we can do this, Lord the girls will be so disappointed. Help me.*

The following week, an official letter from the IRS arrived. My heart sank, but soon, the contents left me speechless. The IRS said our previous quarter's taxes had been overpaid. Enclosed was a refund—the exact amount of a camper I'd seen in the local paper!

Tears welled up. It wasn't just the money, but the timing. This wasn't a coincidence; it was an answer to my prayer. With newfound confidence, I showed Doug the letter. To my surprise, he didn't argue. "See, I told you you'd find a way," he remarked with a smile.

Over the years, as I've reflected on how God provided, I've realized He doesn't always provide in the way I expect. But He always provides. When I meet overwhelming situations, I am reminded that if He can orchestrate an electric bill and the IRS, He can handle whatever I am currently facing. I simply need to ask Him. I need to put my trust in His care for me.

Even when the budget seemed impossible. All it took was a little beans-and-rice desperation prayer and a well-timed overpayment to show me the way.

* * *

Cynthia Martin is a Christian speaker, author, and spiritual growth coach, serving those who want more of God in their life. She has served as a pastoral counselor for twenty-four years, providing in person and online ministry for individuals or groups (CynthiaMartin.org). Cynthia loves to read, research, and eat out.

Questions for Personal Reflection or Group Discussion

In this story, a wife struggles with financial frustrations despite her family's savings. She prays for God's guidance in moments of need, and miraculously, He answers her through an unexpected credit on her electric bill and a perfectly timed refund from the IRS. Over time, Cynthia realizes that while God's provision may not always look the way she expects, He is always faithful to provide.

1. How do you trust God to provide for your needs, even when things seem tight or uncertain?
2. Have you ever experienced an answer to prayer that came in an unexpected or surprising way?
3. How does this story encourage you to bring your daily struggles, even financial ones, to God in prayer?

We pray that Cynthia's story will remind you that God cares about every detail of your life, even your financial concerns. May it encourage you to trust in His provision, knowing that He has a way of meeting your needs, sometimes in ways you least expect. Let this testimony inspire you to place your worries in His hands, trusting that He will provide for you in His perfect timing.

LET'S PRAY TOGETHER

BY PAMELA JANNARONE SCOTT

*F*amilies who pray together stay together. I close my eyes to meditate and travel back in time to precious memories of my family praying together through all seasons of our lives.

Most family members have passed away since then, and I still pray to God for them. Ironically, I am surprised by the signs acknowledging my prayers. I find coins, feathers, visiting cardinals, and I feel the same warmth in my heart of those times we prayed together.

Praying is an intimate connection we have with God. He hears our prayers. Praying keeps us in constant communication with God. He is always there, right beside us. We are family.

There were times when our prayers weren't answered right away, yet the perfect answer is always fulfilling, like a joy and a comfort so rewarding.

One day, my world crumbled as I learned that my mother's mother, my very special grandmother, was not coming home from outpatient surgery. Instead, they were sending her to a nursing and rehabilitation center. She had tripped and fallen in her home and was in need of an immediate shoulder replacement.

For some reason, I couldn't fathom how such a serious injury and proposed surgery could be treated as an outpatient procedure. We prayed for success in her surgery, and for her to come home safe.

Our grandmother was so very special and loved us each in her own special way. Like God, she was the light of our life shining upon us through Him. Prayer gels our family together, and she is the glue bonding us.

At age nine, she endured eleven dark years growing up during the Great Depression. Her mother passed away of breast cancer when she was only three years of age. She would tell me the stories of how she was treated unfairly by her wicked aunt who preferred to raise boys instead of girls. I could tell that she would never forget the dark times in her life. But through prayer and perseverance, she fulfilled her life through the guidance of God's love and light and shared it with us, instilling it in us.

As soon as I learned of my grandmother's transition, I went to visit.

Soon after, I learned the patients at her facility were getting sick and being sent off to the hospital. Some came back, and some did not. I got an eerie feeling about this place and prayed to God without ceasing.

On a particular visit, I questioned the nurse giving my grandmother medications and asked what each pill was. My mother had a list of her prescribed medications that she took normally, but one medication in the nurse's hand was not on the list.

I called her doctor the same day, inquiring about the new medicine and the side effects. The doctor replied that he hadn't prescribed it, and that one of the side effects was memory loss. My grandmother was, indeed, lethargic and out of touch.

Then we learned that her medical insurance would soon run out, and that there was an ultimatum to give up her home to pay for her continued stay there. We demanded to bring her home. God answered our prayers, and she was soon home safe.

We learned two weeks later that the establishment shut down due to a mold problem. Remaining patients were relocated throughout the state.

Years have passed since then as she dwells in the house of the Lord forever. I praise God every day for my grandmother. She shared a deep appreciation of God's love and light through prayer. I continue to pass down to my next generations her love, values, traditions, and spirituality. And we continue to pray through all seasons of life. Praise God. Hallelujah!

* * *

Pamela Jannarone Scott is published in the Christian Writers for Life anthologies *Experiencing God's Presence* and *Hope for Wounded Hearts*. As an English major, she holds a bachelor's degree in liberal arts from Ashford University. She enjoys spending precious time with her family, writing short stories, painting, crocheting, and gardening.

Questions for Personal Reflection or Group Discussion

Pamela shares the story of her family's prayer life, especially during a difficult time when her grandmother's health was at risk. Through prayer, perseverance, and God's guidance, they were able to bring her grandmother home from a dangerous situation. Prayer had always been the foundation of their family, binding them together, and Pamela continues to pass down those values to future generations.

1. How has prayer helped you or your family through difficult or uncertain times?
2. How can Pamela's story encourage you to pray persistently, even when answers are delayed or unclear?

3. What role does prayer play in keeping your family connected, and how can you make prayer a regular part of your life?

We pray that Pamela's story will remind you of the power of family prayer and how it can guide, protect, and sustain you through all seasons of life. May it encourage you to make prayer a priority, trusting that God hears and answers in His perfect timing. Let this testimony inspire you to pass on the importance of prayer to the next generation, just as Pamela's grandmother did, so that faith and connection with God continue to grow.

SURVIVING HUMAN TRAFFICKING

BY DAVID SOLOMON

*I*f someone were to say to me that God does not make miracles happen in today's world, then to help them believe, in faith, I would share this story.

On January 12, 2012, I was just eighteen years old when my mom was given two months to live. On the way to her chemo appointment, I was chloroformed, abducted, and kidnapped. I was taken by some members of the church who had been warned that my mom was sick, and that because she was sick with cancer, her immune system wasn't capable of receiving visitors. But they didn't listen and showed up anyway, continuing with their plans to kidnap me.

For two and a half weeks I was missing, and horrible things happened to me. They took me to their home in Grants Pass, Oregon. When I wanted to go back to my mom, they flashed government paperwork showing guardianship, and the cops released me back into their care. They tried to have me arrested, but their plan failed.

I soon found out that before they kidnapped me, these people had legally changed my name so that when my mom filed a missing person's report, the names wouldn't match.

When I made this discovery, the people decided that it was too risky to keep me in Grants Pass, so they took me to some family members' home in Des Moines, Washington, where I was held for another week. Sometime after, I woke up in a warehouse in Canada with only vague memories of being transported over the border. I was so drowsy that I wasn't fully functioning.

Finally, on January 29, 2012, as I sat in a cage, I prayed for a way out to see my mom again. Soon after I prayed, an angel appeared, and my cage inexplicably opened on its own. I knew God was there with me in that moment, and I knew I had to run.

I found some cash on the counter, along with a credit card, and took off running. It wasn't my proudest moment, but I did what I had to do to make it back to my mom alive. I flagged down a truck driver who offered to drop me off at the Greyhound bus station and refused anything in return.

After a long journey from another country, I made it back to my mom in Oregon. When I returned home, I was shocked to find that she was no longer sick from cancer.

A week later, we returned to the doctor, and he stated that we had survived two miracles: first, my mom was not showing any signs of cancer and didn't need chemo anymore, and second, I had survived human trafficking and made it back home alive.

God had answered my prayers.

So, if someone says to me that God does not make miracles happen today, I know they are wrong. I have lived through many miracles, these being just two examples. God is even working on miracles now as we speak.

This is why I became a writer—to show the miracles He is working each and every day.

* * *

David Solomon is a survivor of human trafficking and carbon monoxide poisoning, and he has been a ghostwriter for various authors in the past. He was called to tell a deeper story of faith to a broken world. You can find David's books on Amazon, and soon in bookstores near you.

Questions for Personal Reflection or Group Discussion

David endured a horrific ordeal of human trafficking, being kidnapped and held captive far from home. In the darkest of moments, he prayed to God, and miraculously, his prayer was answered and he escaped. Upon returning home, David discovered a second miracle: his mother, previously dying of cancer, was healed. These experiences deepened David's faith and his belief in God's ongoing work in the world.

1. How does David's story encourage you to trust in God's miracles, even when life feels hopeless?
2. Have you ever experienced or witnessed a moment where God answered a desperate prayer?
3. How can David's story inspire you to pray and trust in God's presence, even in the most difficult circumstances?

We pray that David's story will remind you that God is still performing miracles today, even in the darkest situations. May it inspire you to trust in His power to heal, protect, and guide you through life's most challenging moments. Let this testimony strengthen your faith, reminding you that God hears every prayer and that miracles can happen, even when you least expect them.

21

WHEN PRAYERS DEFLECT STORMS

BY KAREN MCMULLIN

*H*urricane Alicia acted like a squirrel bouncing from tree to tree in a park, trying to decide which way to go. Would we have a direct hit or would it take its path through Galveston to Houston? We listened to the radio after we had prepared for the storm. The radio report kept changing: first, it said the storm was coming straight for us, then a little while later, it said it was headed to Galveston. The reports wavered back and forth.

A couple of weeks earlier, I was at a Bible study in the same house where we took refuge. As we ended the time together and prayed, the storm was brewing out in the Atlantic Ocean. I closed our prayer time holding hands around the kitchen table and prayed for angels to be around our little coastal town with linked arms just as we stood together in unity. Jesus spoke to the winds and waves to be still (Matthew 8:26). My faith was only large enough to ask for a hedge of protection for our location.

We owned a shrimp boat that my husband took upriver to a turning basin where a deckhand weathered the storm on board to adjust the ropes as the tides fluctuated during the storm. We lived in a house overlooking Matagorda Bay where we also docked our boat. After we boarded up the house, we took our young family to stay with a friend and her children who lived in town. My daughter was not even three months old.

Jan, my friend, and I stood in the middle of the street and made a plan. Her aunt lived in a house across the highway that had three stories and had weathered many storms. So, the tentative plan was to go there with our children if the storm surge came over the dike.

The winds whipped through the trees like a wild animal unleashed from its cage. Yet still, the radio weather reports would be so conflicting as the storm developed into a Category 3 hurricane headed for Texas. Truly, it seemed that the angels were where we had asked them to be, creating a hedge and barrier around our town as the storm bounced off them. God was with us and gave us total peace as we trusted Him and worshiped.

If I had evacuated, I would have gone to my sister's house in Houston. That is where I went three years earlier, prior to having children, prior to having storm-chasing faith. We had a smaller shrimp boat at that time, and my husband took it upriver and tied it to some trees. He remained with the *Lady Alice* during that storm.

This time, my husband drove about twenty miles inland to check on the *Karen Renee* shrimp boat one more time before hunkering down to wait out the storm. All was well at the turning basin where many boats were docked.

Secure in the little red house in our coastal town, we waited and listened to the radio. Hurricane Alicia bounced off our angelic hedge and drove right through downtown Houston. She was a Category 3 storm when she came through Galveston and blew out high-rise building windows all over the city of Houston.

As years have passed, we have grown our faith, and today we pray over the Texas coast from the Rio Grande River to the

Sabine River. We don't wait until there is a disturbance in the Atlantic Ocean headed our way.

We start even before hurricane season begins.

* * *

Karen McMullin is a seasoned Bible teacher. She helps women to grow spiritually by discovering who God is through Bible study, learning to hear God in the quiet of life, and getting answers to prayer through faith. Connect with Karen at her website, https://karen-mcmullin.com for 3.2.1 Encouragement.

Questions for Personal Reflection or Group Discussion

Karen shares a story of faith during Hurricane Alicia as she prayed for protection over her small coastal town. Despite the storm's uncertainty, Karen and her family experienced peace as they trusted God to provide a hedge of protection. Her prayer, like the angels she envisioned, acted as a barrier, keeping the storm from directly hitting their town.

1. How does Karen's prayer for protection during the storm inspire you to trust God in times of uncertainty and danger?
2. Have you ever prayed for protection or deliverance during a difficult situation? How did you experience God's presence during that time?
3. Karen's story emphasizes the importance of praying in advance, even before challenges arise. How can you incorporate this proactive approach to prayer in your own life, trusting God to guide and protect you before storms (literal or figurative) come your way?

We pray that Karen's story will remind you of the power of prayer and the peace that comes when we trust God to guard and protect us. Just as Karen prayed for a hedge of angels around her town, may you also approach God with bold prayers, trusting in His ability to provide safety, guidance, and peace through any storm.

22

PRAYER: A KEY TO OUR HIDDEN TREASURES

BY YOLISA MAPISA

*W*hen we pray, we can easily utter with confidence the statement "I'm not afraid of tomorrow, because I know God is already there," knowing that whatever we need in life has already been provided for.

My story, like that of most of the young people in our community, transpired after graduation. By the time, I was at varsity, and there was no one at home working. We relied on my dad's part-time jobs and disability grant. By God's grace, I managed to get provision and graduated with an honors degree.

After varsity, I had to look for a job so that I could manage to assist at home. I started volunteering at church as a secretary, and at a children's home and at schools as a peer educator. I did anything that had to be done by an administrator without expecting any payment.

At the end of the year, I was offered a job as the church administrator. In 2004, I decided to enter the ministry and went to Creare Ministries International. At the end of 2004, I returned home without a job. I continued as the peer educator and visited homes, schools, and some of the churches that we toured when I was in Creare. I became a volunteer computer teacher for and assisted teachers with extramural activities.

In October of 2006, my dad was involved in an accident and, sadly, passed away. I had to trust God entirely. I drafted my CV again and prayed over it before submitting it to various career sites.

In February of 2007, I received a call from Tupperware; they were offering me a job as a secretary. My skills broadened, and in the same month, my CV was selected by a recruiter for a job interview at Department of Justice. A month later, I was offered a job as a stenographer.

As I adjusted well, God opened more doors for me. I noticed job posts for PAs at the Limpopo Department of Agriculture. I applied for some of those posts, and within a month, I received a call requesting me to come for an interview. I secured the position, and in May, I submitted my resignation letter to the Department of Justice and soon joined the LDA team. To this day, I still work there.

The Bible says that worry robs you of your happiness, but that kind words will cheer you up. It's important not to worry, even if you do not see the way out of your situation. Continue to pray and trust God for a breakthrough. That is what I did.

When praying, surrender all your worries to God—everything that is in your heart. He is always there for you, and He will not lie and will never leave you confused. Do not carry the burden on your shoulders. Lay all your supplications before God and cast your anxieties on Him. God has promised us that He will never leave us nor forsake us, so invite Him and give your burdens to Him.

* * *

Yolisa Mapisa is an alumna of Creare Ministries International where she studied drama, music, and writing. She dedicates her spare time to volunteering at an orphanage, and she writes short stories for children's skits.

Questions for Personal Reflection or Group Discussion

Yolisa's story is a powerful testimony of trusting in God's provision through prayer, even in times of uncertainty. After graduating, she struggled to find stable work but continued volunteering and trusting God. Through prayer and perseverance, doors opened in unexpected ways, leading to a fulfilling career. Yolisa reminds us of the importance of laying all our worries and burdens before God and trusting Him completely.

1. How does Yolisa's story encourage you to rely on God's provision, even when you don't see a clear path ahead?
2. Have you ever experienced a situation where trusting in God through prayer opened unexpected opportunities?
3. How can this story inspire you to surrender your worries and anxieties to God, trusting that He will guide you through life's challenges?

We pray that Yolisa's story will encourage you to trust in God's faithfulness, knowing that He hears your prayers and has a plan for your life. May it inspire you to surrender your burdens, pray without ceasing, and trust God's timing and guidance. Let this testimony remind you that God is always present, ready to lead you through every difficulty and into the plans He has prepared for you.

23

HOMELESS WITH CHRIST

BY KASSANDRA OWENS

I applied for college in September 2022 and suddenly became homeless on October 1, 2022. My auntie kicked me out via text message while I was at church. Unfortunately, it's as bad as it sounds.

Who would kick someone out knowing they had nowhere else to go? And via *text message*? Apparently, a neighbor lied about me, and my auntie believed her but never talked to me about it, so I had no idea what was going on behind the scenes. My cousin, her daughter, told me about it weeks later, and I wanted to talk with my auntie, but she didn't want to talk to me.

The next day, while I was at church, she sent me a long text message saying all the reasons why she didn't want me in her home (there were two reasons, and one of them was a lie). I broke down in tears, and my church family gave me a new definition of the word *family*.

I had only known them for about a month or so, and up until that point, I only worshipped and served the Lord with them. That day, though, many of them circled around me, showered me with hugs and encouraging words, and offered to help me reconcile things with my auntie. I was so deeply hurt and angry with my auntie that I didn't want to ever see her again, so I politely and honestly denied their offer to take me back to her home.

One church member opened her own home to me so I wouldn't have to sleep outside. I was surprised because I had never met her before, but I had met and served with her auntie. I said "yes," and we finished the rest of our fellowship meal with me in bouts of tears as we got to know each other.

On my first night of homelessness, I slept at my new church cousin's apartment. She offered to let me spend the day with her and stay another night at her place, but I felt a strong urge to "go at it alone." She was hesitant but eventually dropped me off at a shelter and left.

I was turned away at that shelter due to overcapacity, so I called the Salvation Army to get a code so that they could pick me up and take me to another shelter. I didn't want to sit around, so I spent that day walking around the east side of Chicago, singing my favorite gospel songs, praying, and eating snacks purchased with my food stamp card.

By the grace of God, I spent the night at Mount Sinai Hospital in their waiting room with a few other homeless people and a security guard. I was approached by two different security guards the next morning, and they told me about a good homeless shelter I could go to. I packed up my snacks and left.

That shelter directed me to 10 S. Kedzie, where I presented my code (the Salvation Army never called) and they expedited my case, registered me for Section 8 housing, interviewed me, and placed me in a Christian-based homeless shelter less than two hours later. I thanked the Lord for guiding me thus far as I walked to Breakthrough Ministries Woman's Shelter.

During my three-month stay there, I was well-received and loved by almost everyone. I got my college acceptance text during my first week of homelessness. Now, in 2024, I'm in Indiana, still attending college and helping the homeless people in my neighborhood. All the glory goes to Him.

* * *

KasSandra Owens is a full-time servant of the Lord and a full-time college student. By the grace of God, she has self-published two eBooks on Amazon entitled *A Peek into My Mind: A Christian Chapbook* (2023) and *A Transformative Approach to Teaching: For All Ages* (2023) with more to come.

Questions for Personal Reflection or Group Discussion

KasSandra faced the harsh reality of becoming homeless unexpectedly, but through it all, she experienced God's provision and the support of her church family. Despite the pain of being rejected by her aunt, KasSandra found strength in her faith, walking with Christ through her homelessness, and she eventually found her way to a supportive Christian shelter. Her journey has since led her to college and a new mission to help others in need.

1. How does KasSandra's story encourage you to trust in God's provision, even when life takes an unexpected turn?
2. Have you ever experienced a situation where a church family or community came together to support you in a time of need?
3. How can KasSandra's story inspire you to help others who may be going through difficult situations, trusting that God is working through you?

We pray that KasSandra's story will remind you that even in the darkest moments, God is always near, providing guidance and help through unexpected ways. May it encourage you to trust in His faithfulness and to lean on the support of your community in times of need. Let this testimony inspire you to be a light to others, just as KasSandra experienced the love and support of her church family, showing how God works through His people.

24

WHEN WE PRAY

BY EDWARD BURCHFIELD

J can truly say that God does answer prayer. I have experienced many miracles in my years since giving my life to Christ. Here is just one of the many, one that happened in 1988 while living in Mobile, Alabama.

My wife, Alden, had been diagnosed with a growth on her ovary. The ultrasound had revealed a tumor about the size of a grapefruit.

This was very fearful in that this would be her tenth surgery in the eighteen years of our marriage. Every surgery had been serious, but the more she had been operated on, the more she was put under anesthesia, and the more danger she faced.

We have been Christians since 1975, and our faith had sustained us through many afflictions, trials, and troubles. This was going to be another affliction, one we were sure God would see us through.

I could sense the fear in my wife, knowing the seriousness of this surgery. The doctor had shared with us there were certain precautions that would have to be taken, and that she could die if they were not.

The surgery was scheduled for a Wednesday morning. I started praying and fasting.

I worked for the highway department, and when I got off work on Monday afternoon, I passed an old man with a sign saying "Pensacola." I felt my heart burn, but I could not pull over due to the traffic. I knew there was something to this old man with the sign, so I prayed, *God if this is from you, let this man be in the same place at the same time tomorrow, and I will stop.*

Well, that is exactly what happened. I pulled over and picked the old gentleman up. I felt the Lord.

This old man immediately started telling me about my wife. He knew things about her that only I knew, and he assured me that everything was going to be alright. I was stunned, to say the least, but encouraged that this was none other than an angel sent by God to reinforce my faith.

I lived toward Pascagoula, Mississippi, but his sign said Pensacola, Florida. I just automatically drove toward my house in Theodore, Alabama, then pulled over and apologized for my mistake.

He said, "Don't worry about it. Thank you for the ride." Again, he said that my wife was going to be alright.

The next morning was Wednesday, the day of the surgery. I told my wife about this mysterious old man and his encouraging words. We prayed and thanked God. The doctor did another sonogram, just to make sure. Sure enough, the tumor was still there. But we believed God.

As the medical personnel wheeled her off to surgery, she waved me goodbye with a smile. I went to the chapel and prayed, thanking God for all He had ever done for us, and for what He was going to do for us.

In an hour or so, the doctor came in. He had a strange look on his face. He said, "I can't explain it—I know it was there from the sonogram—but when I went in, there was nothing there." I told him I have been praying, and he said, "Well, it worked."

GOD ANSWERS OUR PRAYERS

I tell you from experience that God truly answers prayer. In a week, my wife was up walking, and in two weeks, it was like nothing had ever happened. Thirty-six years later, I am still in amazement of this answer to prayer.

* * *

Edward Burchfield was born in 1950 in Bessemer, Alabama. He served nine years in the Army during Vietnam. He was saved in 1975 and is now an evangelist, a chaplain, and an ordained minister. He is a published author and an active member of several writing groups.

Questions for Personal Reflection or Group Discussion

Edward shares a powerful testimony of how prayer and faith saw him and his wife through a difficult time. After his wife was diagnosed with a serious tumor, Edward prayed and fasted, trusting in God's healing power. The mysterious encounter with an old man, who seemed to be a messenger of God, reinforced his faith, and in the end, the tumor miraculously disappeared.

1. How does Edward's story inspire you to trust God during times of uncertainty or fear?
2. Have you ever experienced a moment where prayer provided you with peace or clarity in a difficult situation? How did it impact your faith?
3. What can you learn from Edward's unwavering belief in God's ability to heal? How can this help strengthen your own prayer life?

We pray that Edward's story encourages you to have faith in God's power to answer prayers, even in situations that seem impossible. God is always at work, listening to our prayers and providing guidance and healing in ways we may not expect. Let this story remind you that no request is too big for God, and through prayer, we can experience His miraculous power.

25

A SERIES OF MIRACLES

BY MARCEY E. STEVENS

$\mathcal{M}$y heart was pounding in my throat. My stomach turned inside out as I listened to the sound of the familiar voice on the other end of the line. *Was it really him?* I could feel goosebumps on my skin. Something ignited inside of me like electricity flowing through my veins. I was excited as we talked for hours like we did when we were teens. We had so much to catch up on; it had been over twenty years since we had last spoken to each other.

Then one night he caught me off guard. He blurted out these life altering words. He said, "I am dying, Marcey. Doctors diagnosed me with a rare nerve disease called Reflex Sympathetic Dystrophy (RSD) in 2006. They told me that at the rate the disease was spreading, I would have five years left to live."

"Wait, what?" I said.

He further explained that RSD caused him to feel like his body was on fire all the time. Many people with this condition are unable to receive proper diagnosis or medical treatment. The suicide rate is high. As I continued to listen, I felt like the bottom dropped out of my world until ...

Late one night, Tom nervously asked, "Marcey, will you marry me?" I melted like butter hearing those words.

"Yes, a thousand times, yes," was my reply. The thought filled me with exuberant joy. I would finally be his wife. I hung up the phone and hit my knees, crying hysterically.

"God," I begged. "I will never remarry. I will give myself fully to missionary work. Please give me more time with Tom." I cried until there were no tears left.

I immediately gave my two weeks' notice at work. I hopped on a plane to California to be by Tom's side and take care of him around the clock. Seeing him again was like a dream come true, and when he held me in his arms, it was even better. But the euphoria was short lived.

Once I arrived, the reality and the weight of my responsibilities set in. At first, life was like an emotional roller coaster. Taking on this new responsibility was sometimes overwhelming and scary. But we were together again, and I had faith that, somehow, we would make it.

After months of research and seeking God's guidance, I had a breakthrough. I found a medical procedure that would help to reset the pain receptors in the body. We had a big problem though: it was extremely expensive, and most insurance companies would not cover it.

More time passed by, and we discovered that the VA in Ohio would perform the procedure cost-free, even though they classified it as experimental. This was a game changer, and the beginning of my husband's recovery—praise God.

Thanks to a series of miracles, we have been living on God's grace for thirteen years. His condition reversed from stage four back to stage one, which was unheard of. We have been able to reduce his medicine by ninety percent. And we have never fought this lengthy battle alone.

To God be all the glory for my husband's magnificent

recovery. God has filled in the gaps of what we could not do. I will forever be grateful to the God of mercy for all He has done for us.

"If you have faith as small as a grain of mustard seed ... nothing shall be impossible to you" (Mathew 17:20-21). Whatever you may be going through, I encourage you to place all your trust, hope, and faith in the God of the impossible! He will never disappoint you.

* * *

Marcey E. Stevens is a Christian minister who is passionate about her relationship with God, prayer, and writing for Jesus Christ. She shares her life experiences of journeying with God, along with her Bible knowledge, to help others to become liberated and more deeply connected to God.

Questions for Personal Reflection or Group Discussion

Marcey faced the devastating news that the man she loved, Tom, had been diagnosed with a terminal nerve disease. However, through prayer, faith, and miraculous interventions, they discovered a treatment that brought about Tom's improved health. Despite the odds, Marcey and Tom have lived with God's grace, witnessing firsthand His power to heal and provide hope.

1. How does Marcey's story encourage you to hold onto faith, even when faced with seemingly impossible circumstances?
2. Have you ever experienced a moment when God provided a miracle or an unexpected answer to prayer?
3. How can Marcey's journey inspire you to trust God fully, knowing that He can fill in the gaps where human effort falls short?

We pray that Marcey's story will remind you of the power of faith in God, even in the face of overwhelming challenges. May it inspire you to trust in God's ability to work miracles and to guide you through difficult situations. Let this testimony encourage you to place your faith in the God of the impossible, knowing that He can bring healing, hope, and grace to every situation.

26

THE RAH-RAH

BY PATRICIA "TRISH" KANIPE

*M*oving to Jacmel, Haiti, my dream was to work with the women and children on the streets. Adapting to a new way of life took time, especially when it came to the abundance of occult activity. Previously, the term *Rah-Rah* elicited memories of fall football and cheerleading, but my Haitian experience instilled in me a different perception.

A Rah-Rah in Haiti is a celebration of someone coming to Satan, much like we might celebrate someone accepting Christ. Rah-Rahs are unpredictable, have a potentially dangerous element, and often lack moral restraint. My first experience was unsettling, particularly given that it turned its attention toward me.

Church services were held under the stars in an open field, and while still learning Creole, I listened intently, hoping to fit enough pieces together to understand the message. One warm, muggy evening, our service was interrupted by the sounds of distant music and chanting. Some in the congregation seemed annoyed, some fretted, but I was naïve and clueless.

The wailing chants weaved their way through the mountain air; it was as if the voices in the distance and the pastor's words were playing verbal volleyball. Finally exasperated, the pastor closed his Bible and started preaching about the power of the blood of Christ. As the pastor spoke, the chants lessened and then grew quiet. What followed was the beginning of an education that I wasn't sure I wanted.

Safely walking home was no longer an option. Driving past the Rah-Rah parade, my ignorance was proven in an eye-popping, jaw-dropping reaction. A few people were mostly naked, and all writhed as if in pain or ecstasy. It was difficult to determine which as they frantically shouted and waved palm fronds in the air.

When I arrived home, I could still hear them from a distance, and I quickly ran into my home. I pressed my back against the door, trying to settle my anxious thoughts and stop my knees from shaking. The chanting grew louder and closer. Were they really walking up my dead-end street, or were fear and imagination causing me to self-destruct? The screaming became overwhelming, and peeking out my window, I got the answer I didn't want. They had stopped in front of my house and turned their attention toward me. I was not new to spiritual warfare, but it was the first time I would encounter a large group and do so alone.

An atmosphere of the presence of evil was thick. I had been warned to avoid walking the street behind my house as it was the location of a satanic temple. I felt sandwiched by evil. In desperation, I dropped to my knees and prayed for wisdom, peace, and protection. My home didn't yet have furniture, and my voice echoed from wall to wall in encouragement. It seemed like an eternity, but the presence of the Rah-Rah slowly dwindled, and my street once again grew quiet.

I awoke several times that night, and each awakening was answered with a loud, determined prayer. Prayer was the one thing that brought peace and settled my soul in truth. Praying reminded me of the authority I had in Christ, and that I was never alone.

The morning light brought about one thought: *So this is Haiti!* Never again did a Rah-Rah stop in front of my house, but I did learn an important lesson that would carry me throughout my days on various mission fields:

Prayer is the answer to all of Satan's lies, and I can peacefully rest in the arms of God regardless of the circumstances.

* * *

Patricia "Trish" Kanipe is a believer, missionary, public speaker, survivor, and artist living in Boone, North Carolina. She is a contributor to *Experiencing God's Presence* and *Hope for Wounded Hearts*. She studied education and psychology and is passionate about missions and teaching the "how-tos" of healing from trauma.

Questions for Personal Reflection or Group Discussion

Trish's powerful story recounts her first encounter with a "Rah-Rah" in Haiti—a chaotic celebration tied to occult practices. Alone and frightened, Trish turns to prayer for peace, protection, and strength. Through her experience, she learns the vital importance of prayer in spiritual warfare and how it affirms her authority in Christ. The story illustrates the power of God's protection and the transformative effect of relying on prayer during overwhelming circumstances.

1. How does Trish's response to fear through prayer inspire you to turn to God when facing intimidating or spiritually challenging situations?
2. Have you ever experienced a situation that felt spiritually overwhelming, where prayer became your lifeline? How did it impact you?

3. Trish talks about being reminded of the authority she has in Christ through prayer. What steps can you take to more fully embrace the authority and power that come from your faith during difficult times?

We pray that Trish's story encourages you to trust in the power of prayer, especially during times of spiritual attack or uncertainty. Remember that God's protection is always present, and prayer is a direct line to His peace and strength.

27

DREAMS

BY KIMBERLY OWEN

*D*reams seem hard to even relate to the older I get. Life has taken a toll on my heart and soul. I am honestly angry when people talk about their dreams all the time. I had dreams when I was young; most of my dreams did not come to pass. For years, I experienced rough patches. Then I remarried and had a family and just got by, day after day.

Currently, I have two teenage girls who prefer friends over parents. So, I decided to start thinking about my life.

For six months, I was sick and couldn't work. I decided to investigate writing courses and copywriting. I have always written, mostly in a journal. I didn't tell anyone, not even my family. Then my birthday came, and my best friend from out of state sent me a bracelet that said *DREAM*. If it had been from anyone else, I would have been mad.

I began pursuing my dream but had to go back to an old job to pay the bills. I went back because I could do the job well, but it wasn't what kept me going every day. Raising my daughters and helping my eldest pursue her dream in crew and going to England for big, well-known race in the was one of my dreams for her, along with my own dream of getting published in magazine or securing a copywriting position in a company.

I started by going back to the basics. I began attending a church and praying daily or even more, depending on what type of day I was having. I told God, *I am all in and will do whatever You ask me to do.* I know that if it's not in God's plan, it will not succeed.

Everything I have been doing is out of my comfort zone. I even sent writing to a Christian magazine and thought, *I doubt will like this but here it is.* Well, the woman in charge told me to keep writing and not listen to people who say I cannot write. I am currently in three separate months of her magazine. I bought copies to see my work in print. This has been a dream of mine since I first became a Christian fifteen years ago.

Also, at about that same time, I came across someone who was looking for volunteers at a non-profit. It was a cause I was passionate about. Within a week's time, I was writing content for this non-profit. I am not making money, but my heart is so happy that I cannot contain myself. The woman at the non-profit loves the work I am doing and wishes I lived closer to visit her sometime.

Guess what? That is now another dream for the next few years. Recently, I went to meeting at our church and decided to email the woman about her non-profit and see if I could help her in anyway. I have a meeting with her this week. God is in control. I did not expect this email to even go this far. I have been honest about my limited experience, but they can see how passionate I am about their organization that they are giving me a shot.

Jeremiah 29:11 has been one of my favorite verses. But, in the two following verses, he says, "We have to call on him and pray to him. Then, you will seek me and find me when you seek me with all your heart."

Fully commit! God can give you your dreams. These dreams may seem impossible, but, with God, all things are possible.

* * *

Kimberly Owen is a mom of two teenagers who has loved to write for her entire life. She has had short stories published in magazines, and this is her first story contest win. She is being led where God wants her to write.

Questions for Personal Reflection or Group Discussion

Kimberly had given up on her dreams as life's hardships took a toll on her heart. But after returning to prayer and committing herself fully to God, she saw doors open that she thought were long closed. As she pursued her dream of writing, she found new opportunities to use her talents, discovering that with God, nothing is impossible.

1. How have life's challenges affected your dreams, and how can you reconnect with them through prayer and trust in God?
2. Have you ever felt like giving up on something, only to see God open a door in an unexpected way?
3. How does Kimberly's story encourage you to fully commit your dreams to God, trusting that He will guide you?

We pray that Kimberly's story will remind you that God cares about your dreams and can bring them to life, no matter how impossible they may seem. May it inspire you to seek Him with all your heart, trusting that His plans for you are good and that He can make a way where there seems to be no way. Let this testimony encourage you to keep pursuing your passions, knowing that God is in control and will lead you to the desires of your heart.

2 8

MIRACULOUS PROVISION

BY MARY MUELLER

I consider myself to be an upbeat and positive person, maybe even a bit of a Pollyanna. Even so, even in my wildest dreams, I *never* thought someone would offer to give my husband and me $60,000 with no strings attached.

We were free will ministers at a small church in Florida. Our denomination had a history of calling people from the congregation to serve as pastors, so when the former pastor resigned, the members prayed for discernment. Five members, including the two of us, were called to share the minister's responsibilities.

We started classes to get licensed and ordained, adding to our busy schedule with our family, work, and volunteering. Within a few months, three of our team resigned because of a concern with a denominational biblical interpretation. That left John and me. We laughingly claimed that God had "tricked" us as we wouldn't have been brave enough to do this if we had known it was only going to be the two of us.

Two years into the process, on a Sunday morning, we got a call from one of the Northern couples who worshipped with us during the winter months. They wanted to talk to us, so we invited them to lunch after the service. We had some trepidation about the meeting, knowing sometimes people got upset over minor things like the pews getting recovered in red rather than blue. Since we had no idea what they wanted, we took a "wait and see" attitude.

Over lunch, the man explained that he and his wife wanted to support our church. He felt we were carrying a heavy load with all that we had on our plate and they wanted to help us. He and his wife pledged a two-year commitment to give us $2,500 every month.

As many things as John and I had thought that this meeting might be about, this wasn't one of them! It all seemed surreal; I felt like the ground had suddenly shifted beneath my feet.

One part of me was excited about their generous offer, knowing how much easier life would be if we accepted, while the other part of me thanked them but explained the ministers' ethics rules: ministers could not accept money from any member of their congregation. They replied that they were not members here; they held membership in their own church.

Seeing that we were still hesitant, they shared their story.

They had been successful in their careers and had acquired some wealth. A few years earlier, they had been asked to financially back a start-up business with the possibility of becoming very wealthy. They prayed and told God that if it worked out, they would donate half of their earnings.

It was successful, and he told us that while he was getting ready that morning, God said, *Well, big mouth, are you going to put your money where your mouth is?* He said God told him to help us, and that is why he was at our table.

We explained that part of our hesitation was that our last pastor had been asked to resign over some money concerns, and as much as we appreciated their offer, we did not want to misstep or cross any boundaries. They persisted in urging us to accept, so we offered a plan: If they received approval from the church board and the district executive, we would be *thrilled* to accept.

They did receive approval and honored their two-year commitment.

The God of miracles blessed us with $60,000, proving that when we heed His calling, He will always provide.

* * *

Mary Mueller, an avid volunteer with Brethren Disaster Ministries, is a mother, grandmother, and great-grandmother. Her children's books, *What Do You Call an Ant?*, *What Did You Bring Me?*, and *How Much Gold Can an Octopus Hold?* can be viewed at her website, authormarymueller.com.

Questions for Personal Reflection or Group Discussion

Mary and her husband, John, were faithfully serving their small church when they received an unexpected offer of financial support from a couple who wanted to bless them. Despite their initial hesitation due to ethical concerns, they saw God's miraculous provision unfold when everything aligned. This blessing was a powerful reminder of how God provides when His people walk in obedience to His calling.

1. How does Mary's story encourage you to trust God's provision, even when you can't see how your needs will be met?
2. Have you ever experienced an unexpected blessing that reminded you of God's care and provision?
3. How can this story inspire you to respond in faith when God calls you to serve, trusting that He will provide for your needs along the way?

We pray that Mary's story will remind you that God always provides for those who faithfully follow His calling. May it encourage you to trust in His provision, knowing that He can work through unexpected people and circumstances to meet your needs. Let this testimony inspire you to remain faithful and open to the ways God may bless you or others in your community, showing His goodness and generosity.

29

PRAYING OVER FINANCES

BY ROSE WALKER

*L*uke 6:38 says, "Give and it shall be given unto you, good measure, pressed down, shaken together, and running ever." Malachi 3:10 defines the tithe as the first tenth of everything we get. According to these two verses, God will bless us if we return to Him what He has asked of us.

In Luke, Jesus used a metaphor of gathering grain into a bushel basket. Harvesters would pack it in the basket, pressing it down, and shaking it around, adding more each time until the grain was falling over the edges.

This illustrates that we cannot out-give God. We cannot give without receiving a blessing. Give things you have—money, time, love, clothes, skills, anything. Give to God. Give to others. Accept gifts given, graciously. Jesus also told us to pray for what we need. We're likely to experience miracles.

For most of my son's high school experience, I'd had to drive him to and from school. He resented this fact, complaining that he was the only senior without his own car and a personally designed parking space. I desperately wanted to, at least, get him into a car of his own for graduation; that didn't happen. But his eighteenth birthday was only a few weeks away. A combination graduation/birthday gift would be good. Yet it seemed to be an impossible goal—the money just wasn't there.

Meanwhile, our cousin was doing missionary work in Africa, and I had wanted to contribute toward her endeavor. During the week before my son's birthday, I wrote a meager tithe check of fifteen dollars and a note to her and placed it in the mailbox, raising the red flag. I made no connection of that gift to the fact that I'd been praying fervently for provision of a cool car for my son as my husband and I searched the internet and local dealerships. We'd found a nice gold Firebird with a T-top at a reasonable price, but it was still more than we could afford.

A couple of hours after placing that little check in the mailbox, I returned to get the day's incoming mail and discovered an envelope containing a $2,000 check. It included a brief note that said, "For Jason's car; pay it forward." It was from one of my best friends, a high school and college classmate and fellow minister's wife. She'd been saving up to replace her own car but didn't need the money for that after another minister friend who'd receive a free car early in his own ministry, decided to pay forward the random act of kindness. She said that God kept telling her to "give the money to Rose," so she did.

We ran to the dealership and were able to make a sizable down payment toward the reasonable price we got for the cool gold Firebird. And we were offered ninety days to figure out how to come up with the remaining balance—even if it meant taking out a loan. I know that all of this happened because, through faith, I'd given a token of fifteen dollars. God returned $2,000—a *very* "good measure, pressed down, shaken together, and overflowing."

The night before my son's eighteenth birthday, we had him come outside to discover his surprise that we had parked in the yard. It had a big bow on it, but it still took him a few seconds to realize what was going on. He swooped up this mama and swung me around. He was ecstatic.

Thank You, Jesus, for providing abundantly via a best friend!

* * *

Rose Walker has published stories in three other Christian Writers for Life anthologies: *Mother, Experiencing God's Presence,* and *Hope for Wounded Hearts,* and on SCWC's blog, along with a poem in *Anchored.* She authored *A Mom's Mentality* and a column/blog entitled "Rose's Remuddlings," and she is working on a children's book.

Questions for Personal Reflection or Group Discussion

Rose and her family were facing financial difficulties, especially as her son Jason longed for a car of his own. Rose prayed fervently for God's provision but wasn't sure how it would happen. After giving a small donation to a missionary, Rose received a surprise—a $2,000 check from a friend, enough to make a down payment on the perfect car for Jason. God's unexpected provision was a powerful reminder of His faithfulness and how even small acts of giving can lead to overwhelming blessings.

1. How does Rose's story of God providing for her son's car encourage you to trust God in your own financial needs?
2. Have you ever experienced a moment where God provided for you in a way that exceeded your expectations, like Rose receiving the check for Jason's car?
3. What does Rose's act of giving, despite her own financial struggles, teach you about the importance of generosity in your relationship with God?

We pray that Rose's story reminds you of the power of prayer and God's ability to provide exactly what you need, sometimes in ways you could never imagine. No prayer is too small or too big for God, and His answers come in His perfect timing, often bringing more blessings than we ever anticipated.

30

HELD IN HIS ARMS

BY SHANA BURCHARD

*T*he ICU lights were dim and the room was quiet. My father lay on the hospital bed, unaware of his surroundings. It was Christmas, but it didn't feel like it. The long days of hospital visits and sleepless nights felt like a heavy fog. The doctors had diagnosed him with meningitis.

I didn't know if my father would ever wake up. Meningitis causes inflammation of the lining around the brain. Even if he did wake up, I didn't know if he would remember me.

My sisters and I took turns giving a Christmas gift to my father, though he slept. But I couldn't speak. My heart was too heavy in my chest. So, I played Christmas music. I let the words of joy cradle me through the dense sadness.

And I still need this today. I still need the words of Jesus to cradle me in times of sickness and health, in joy and sorrow, and with others and alone. I still need to remember what God's Word says is true so that I can carry on.

Every word of God is perfect. My heart captures the words like a hungry child. My father was in the hospital, but my Heavenly Father was always there, listening to the cries of my heart. He was speaking words of truth, and He continues to speak them when my heart wants to give up. Even in a world ridden with sorrow, perfect love has always embraced me. Even though God may have felt far away, He has never left my side.

Day after day, I prayed for my father along with the body of Christ. God heard our prayers and healed my father. He came out of his sleep-like state, and I praised God that his mind was intact. He remembered me.

It is a beautiful gift from God to be remembered and known in the eyes of those you love most. My heart still bears the etching of the sorrows from that year.

But it causes me to remember—to remember God's goodness through a hard season. To remember to be cradled by His love in His words. And to pray without ceasing.

I look back at that winter, and I never want to go through that season again. I can feel tears starting as I write you this. But I know, dear reader, that God loves you. You may think He forgot you, but He has never forgotten you or stopped loving you.

In Matthew, it says, "Look at the birds of the air: they neither sow nor reap nor gather into barns, and yet your Heavenly Father feeds them. Are you not of more value than they?" (Matthew 6:26). I am reminded that my life, and my father's, are precious in His eyes. The sin and destruction of this world cause intense sadness, but my God is a giver of good gifts. He desires healing and reconciliation. It doesn't always happen the way we want or expect. Sometimes the answer is to wait. And sometimes, I just need to be held by my Heavenly Father and rest in His perfect love.

Now, each Christmas, I am forever reminded of what God brought my family through. Every smile, every hug, every word spoken is a testament to God's grace. A testament to His goodness. And I walk in that humble reminder that I am cradled by His love. Will you turn your heart toward Him and let Him cradle you?

* * *

Shana Burchard, an award-winning writer from Pennsylvania, has a passion for quality Christian literature. When she's not writing, she enjoys taking walks outside and coffee dates. She earned English and psychology degrees from Allegheny College, along with a master's degree in education from Mercyhurst University. Follow her at https://linktr.ee/shburns7.

Questions for Personal Reflection or Group Discussion

Shana faced the deep sadness of watching her father battle meningitis in the ICU, not knowing if he would wake up or recognize her. As she prayed and relied on God's Word for comfort, she experienced the peace of being held in His arms. Her prayers were answered when her father was healed, reminding Shana of God's love and goodness through difficult seasons.

1. How can you find comfort in God's love and promises when you are faced with fear or uncertainty?
2. Have you experienced a time when you felt held by God's presence during a difficult situation? How did it change your perspective?
3. How does Shana's story encourage you to trust that God is with you, even when the situation seems overwhelming or hopeless?

We pray that Shana's story will remind you that God is always near, holding you in His arms, especially in times of sorrow or fear. May it encourage you to trust in His perfect love and to find comfort in His promises, knowing that He hears your prayers and walks with you through every season of life. Let this testimony inspire you to lean on God's Word, trusting that His goodness and grace will carry you, no matter what challenges you face.

CONSTANT CONTACT

BY NANCY LEE BETHEA

*P*rayer for me is an ongoing conversation with God. Yes, I try to set aside time every morning to work through my requests for our world, our nation, my family members, and my concerns. But in my daily life, I live in constant contact with God.

One July a few years ago, my husband took our daughter and me to Sanibel Island on Florida's Gulf Coast for a work conference. He attended sessions during the day, but in the evenings, we played on the island's lush beaches, found pristine shells and sand dollars, and watched the colorful coastal birds.

One evening at sunset, we headed to the beach after dinner. The orange and pink streaks in the sky reflected on the calm water. My daughter and I waded far from the shore in the shallow water. I stopped when the water was waist deep, while my daughter swam and enjoyed underwater views through her mask. While we splashed, my husband explored the shore, photographing the picturesque Florida landscape.

The moment personified peace, beauty, and relaxation. We floated, jumped, and flipped in the water.

Then, in the evening light, I saw a shiny silver fin swim toward us, and then another, and then another. We were too far from the shore to return there quickly. I considered calling for my husband, but he had disappeared into a photographer's beach paradise. He would never hear us.

Sharks! I thought.

I shifted quickly in the direction of my daughter, praying as I reached for her.

My prayer, one of those quick, stream-of-consciousness shots to Heaven, went something like, *Lord, protect us!*

By then, there were five or six fins forming a circle around us. My daughter slipped under water before I got to her and popped up with a huge snaggle-toothed smile on her masked face.

"Mommy, they're-"

"We have to get to shore! Now!" I said.

"Mommy," she said happily. "They're dolphins!"

Still uneasy, I looked around. Could she be right? Had the Lord protected us and given us a swim with dolphins to boot?

My daughter surfaced again, giggling this time. "You can hear them! Go under water, Mommy!"

I prayed again, asking for God to guard us.

"Go under, Mommy," she said.

Moving forward in faith, I plunged underneath the surface of the water. Immediately, I heard high-pitched squeaks and peeps as dolphins encircled us. I don't know what they were saying to each other, but it was definitely a conversation!

Maybe the dolphins were communicating to the Creator of the universe through prayer like I had only moments earlier.

We swam with the dolphins for probably five minutes. Then, my daughter and I watched them form a line and swim away into the sunset.

"Thank You, Lord," I whispered as they left.

God had not only answered my prayer for immediate protection, but He had given us a delightful and memorable moment.

I know God doesn't always answer our prayers in such dramatic and instantaneous ways, but this moment and others like it remind me I can stay in constant contact with Him.

* * *

Nancy Lee Bethea is a professional writer and educator who lives in Florida with her husband, her daughter, and the family's rescue cat. She loves to use her words to write uplifting pieces for audiences young and old.

Questions for Personal Reflection or Group Discussion

Nancy shares a story of how her ongoing conversation with God—prayer—brought peace and protection in a moment of uncertainty. While wading in the waters of Sanibel Island with her daughter, Nancy noticed fins swimming toward them, leading her to believe they were in danger. After a quick, desperate prayer, she realized the "sharks" were actually dolphins, and the experience turned into an awe-inspiring moment of swimming with the friendly creatures. This story shows the power of staying connected with God through prayer, even in the everyday moments of life.

1. How does Nancy's story encourage you to incorporate prayer into your daily life, not just during formal times of worship or devotion?
2. Have you ever had a moment of fear or uncertainty that turned into a blessing after you prayed? What was that experience like?
3. What can you learn from Nancy's example of "constant contact" with God, especially during stressful or unexpected moments?

We pray that Nancy's story will inspire you to stay connected with God in all circumstances, trusting that He is always with you and ready to answer your prayers, even in the most unexpected ways. Whether you're facing a joyful moment or a challenging one, remember that God is just a prayer away.

32

SEEKING A SIGNPOST

BY JANET SHEARER

*T*he tears streamed down my face. I crossed my arms over the knot in my stomach. *Dear God, please show us the path for Mary Kate.*

My husband, our daughter, and I had recently returned from her junior year's spring break college tour. The last stop was a large, midwestern university with a highly ranked ballet program.

We observed ballet class, toured the first-rate facilities, and visited with the artistic director. Graduates of the program enjoyed professional careers with dance companies across the US. On her Instagram, Mary Kate posted a photo of herself at the limestone gates of the beautiful campus. Her caption declared her aspirations and echoed our desire for her to study there.

According to university statistics, over 300 ballet dancers auditioned each year for the program. The school accepted fifteen. Was Mary Kate good enough? That question and many others disturbed the peace of my early morning walk.

Were my husband and I crazy to encourage her pursuit of ballet? Would she be brokenhearted if she did not get into a top-tier program? Would she be able to find work, be financially stable after college?

And what of her walk with God? How does a parent prepare a child for a career in a field seemingly wrought with negative social pressures?

At age three, Mary Kate had held my hand as we exited the theater following a session of the USA International Ballet Competition where top dancers vied for company contracts. "I want to do that," she said.

Although academically inclined, Mary Kate worked harder at ballet than anything else. Our daughter had been gifted in this art form. Her dancing brought joy and reflected God's image through creativity. Our society needed Christians making art more than ever.

I felt as if I were on a long hike in unfamiliar woods, wondering if I were even on the trail. I continued my prayer, *Dear Lord, please give me a sign that we are going in the right direction.*

A few weeks later my husband, daughter, and I attended an annual ballet festival. The artistic director we met during spring break had not attended the festival before. However, that year he was teaching and participating in the college recruitment program.

After the college recruitment class, the director asked Mary Kate, "Are you coming to audition for me?'

Mary Kate's eyes widened at the invitation to apply. "Yes, sir."

"Good," he said, giving me the first sign of God's direction for her since my emboldened prayer.

Barely a week later, Mary Kate received an email from a director at a second university. He wrote, "I enjoyed watching your work at the festival last weekend. You show a lot of promise … . Our graduates are performing and teaching nationally and internationally in respected professional companies and schools. Although we only admit about fifteen dancers per year, from what I saw, you would be a great fit for our program."

Mary Kate attended a summer intensive at the university we had visited during spring break. The week-long program ended with a performance for parents. "Mary Kate has her own spark, her own fire," the director said to us, admiring her work ethic and spirit. Echoing the invitation of the director, another faculty member asked, "You are coming to audition for us, aren't you?"

Like blazes along a forest trail, God had provided not one but three signposts in the span of as many months. We were not at the destination, but God had assured us that we were on the path.

* * *

Janet Shearer is a Mississippi writer and artist, documenting and painting a creative life. She and her husband, Dale, have two children. Mary Kate is a professional ballerina and Sam is a writer and filmmaker. Janet's artwork and writing can be found at janetdshearer.com.

Questions for Personal Reflection or Group Discussion

Janet shares her family's emotional journey as they sought direction for their daughter Mary Kate's future in ballet, a highly competitive and demanding field. Through prayer and seeking God's guidance, they received three distinct signposts—affirmations from ballet professionals—that confirmed they were on the right path. The story shows how God answers prayers for guidance and reassures us when we feel uncertain about the future.

1. How does Janet's story encourage you to seek God's guidance when you are unsure of the path ahead, especially in important decisions?
2. Can you think of a time when you asked God for a sign or direction and received confirmation, like Janet's family did? How did it strengthen your faith?

3. What can you learn from this story about the importance of trusting God even when you're in the middle of the journey and haven't yet reached the destination?

We pray that Janet's story reminds you that God often provides signposts along the way, offering reassurance and guidance when we seek Him. Trusting in His direction, even when we haven't reached the final destination, can fill us with peace and confidence that we are walking the right path.

33

GOD'S SENSE OF HUMOR AND MY RESTFUL BREAK

BY SANDEE GILLER

*O*wning a courier business with my husband, Scott, was like being on a never-ending roller coaster. For the first five or six years, we worked 365 days a year, never slowing down. Exhausted and desperate, I found myself praying, *God, please give us a break. We need rest!*

In my close relationship with God, I like to think of Him as having a great sense of humor. Little did I know, He had a rather amusing way of answering my prayer. One day, I noticed it was becoming painful to sit or walk for any length of time. The pain worsened until my chiropractor sent me for an MRI, which revealed a "ginormous" tumor in my uterus. And just like that, I was bedridden for the next five months.

When I first heard the news about the tumor, surprisingly, I felt no fear. Instead, I chuckled and thought, "Well, God, you really do have a great sense of humor." It was clear to me that this was His unconventional way of giving me the rest I had desperately prayed for.

Meanwhile, Scott was left to run our courier business almost single-handedly. Thankfully, our friends rallied around us, helping with deliveries and other tasks. From my bed, I managed the paperwork side of the business.

We reached out to a surgeon to remove the tumor, but he wouldn't operate until I had back surgery to address my mobility issues. The back surgeon, however, wouldn't operate until the tumor was removed. This catch-22 dragged on for five months. Each trip to the doctor's office was a painful ordeal, taking me thirty minutes just to get from the bedroom to the car. Thankfully, our single-story home made this somewhat manageable.

God's provision was evident in many ways. We had an old 1977 Chrysler Town & Country Wagon, affectionately known as our "land yacht." I could crawl in from the back and lie down during the ride to doctors' appointments. To avoid unnecessary and painful trips, we started faxing my story to doctors, asking them to inform us if they weren't comfortable doing the surgery.

During this challenging time, friends and acquaintances from our church and Sunday school were a constant source of support. They visited me, brought meals, and my chiropractor even made house calls to adjust me and help me shower. Scott hosted a men's Bible study at our house where the group prayed over me. Despite everything, people were amazed at my good spirits. I would always say, "God is answering my prayer for rest. It might not be my idea of rest, but He still answered my prayers." I shared how this special time with friends wouldn't have happened if I wasn't going through this season.

Five months into this ordeal, we were referred to a doctor specializing in uterine fibroid tumors. As soon as he saw the MRI results, he said, "What's the problem? The tumor has to come out." A week later, the surgery was done. The tumor ended up being close to thirty-five pounds. The doctor retired one week after my six-week check-up.

Throughout this period, there were many answered prayers. God's provision, the unwavering support of our friends, and the lessons learned about trust and reliance on Him turned this challenging time into a profound testament to His faithfulness. While many would view this as a trial, it only deepened and strengthened my trust and relationship with God. I know with certainty that I can do all things through Christ Jesus.

* * *

Sandee Giller, an entrepreneur from Belmont, New Hampshire, teaches Canva, explores New England, and enjoys cooking with her husband. She is passionate about faith and gratitude, sharing her inspiring stories through writing and social media.

Questions for Personal Reflection or Group Discussion

Sandee recounts how her prayer for rest from the exhausting demands of running a courier business was answered in an unexpected way when she was diagnosed with a tumor, leaving her bedridden for five months. While the situation was challenging, Sandee embraced God's sense of humor and saw His provision in every aspect of the journey—from the support of friends and family to the eventual surgery that restored her health. Sandee's story beautifully illustrates how God answers prayers in ways we might not anticipate, and how faith can carry us through the most difficult of times.

1. How does Sandee's experience of seeing humor and God's provision in a difficult situation inspire you to trust God's plan, even when the answer to your prayers doesn't come in the way you expect?
2. Have you ever prayed for something and felt that God's answer came in an unexpected or even amusing way, like Sandee's "rest"? How did that experience shape your faith?

3. What can we learn from Sandee's ability to maintain a positive attitude and trust in God, even when her situation seemed overwhelming?

We pray that Sandee's story encourages you to look for God's hand at work in every season of life, trusting that He hears and answers prayers in His own perfect and sometimes humorous way. Let her story remind you to find joy and faith even in the midst of trials, knowing that God's provision is always present.

34

LEARNING TO PRAY ... GOD'S WAY

BY PETER HONG

There are four things I cannot afford to lose: my phone, my keys, my wallet, and—I can't remember the fourth, but if I lose any of the other three, I'm sure to lose my mind.

Yet here I was in the all too familiar posture of panic, having lost my wallet. I drove back to the last place I remembered holding it. Having searched the area as thoroughly as I could at twilight, I came to the obvious conclusion: it was lost, God only knew where.

Since only God knew where my wallet was, I began praying feverishly—the way I do when I'm praying as a last resort. As I drove, incoherent thoughts in my mind translated into even less coherent words coming off my lips. Thankfully, God saw through my panic and reminded me of a similar incident only months earlier.

I was "living homeless" as part of a mission trip in San Diego. We spent a week on the streets— no hotels, no cards or cash, living on little more than God's provision to survive. It gave us "street cred" with the homeless people whom we would meet, engage, and pray for.

There was one small caveat: the pastor who led the trip brought along his wallet with an "emergency" credit card. Sure enough, our emergency arose when the wallet with the card (and the pastor's ID) went missing. We prayed. We searched. We prayed. No wallet.

I remembered the pastor's prayer. It was not a prayer I ever prayed: "Lord, You know where my wallet is and Your plans for it. While I'd really like to have my ID and credit card back, if You want a homeless person to have it, let them put it to good use. Amen."

Amen? That was it … nothing about the credit card the pastor needed for his upcoming mission trip to Central America, not to mention the ID he would need to board a plane in two days? Remembering the sheer audacity of the prayer pushed the panic out of my head.

Then, another prayer came to my mind: "Your will be done … on Earth as it is in Heaven." It was one of those prayers I had mindlessly repeated so many times that it was more a line or a mantra than a prayer. Did I really want God's will to be done, or was I asking Him to make sure that my will be done?

Arriving home, I was filled with a peace that would have made no sense just minutes before. Instead of the frantic thoughts that had hijacked my mind like a computer virus, I could think coherently, knowing that my wallet and I were both in God's hands. Most importantly, I could say with confidence, "Lord, Your will be done. Amen."

My phone rang (I hadn't lost that). It was the police department. An anonymous person had turned in my wallet, and could I come pick it up. As I started my car (I hadn't lost my keys either), I remembered Isaiah 55:9:

> "For as the heavens are higher than the earth,
> so are my ways higher than your ways
> and my thoughts than your thoughts."

I've got your back. Do you really need to know how?
Amen.

* * *

Peter Hong is a writer and attorney living in northern Virginia. His ministry interests include evangelism, mission work, and restorative justice. The eldest son of Korean immigrants, Mr. Hong grew up in Newport News, Virginia, and earned degrees at Carleton College, Georgetown University Law Center, and the George Washington University.

Questions for Personal Reflection or Group Discussion

Peter found himself panicking after losing his wallet, only to be reminded of a past experience where he had learned a new way to pray, trusting God's will rather than his own desires. Through this experience, Peter realized the power of surrendering to God's plans, and the peace that comes from trusting God, even in seemingly small challenges. In the end, God provided, returning his wallet through an anonymous person.

1. When you face challenges, do you find it hard to pray for God's will instead of your own desires?
2. How does Peter's story encourage you to trust God in both big and small moments of uncertainty?
3. Have you ever experienced a time when God gave you peace in a situation where you would normally feel anxious or worried?

We pray that Peter's story will remind you of the power of trusting God's will in every situation, no matter how big or small. May it inspire you to surrender your concerns to Him, knowing that His ways are higher than ours. Let this testimony encourage you to trust that God is always in control, and that He cares for you in every detail of your life.

35

HOPE FULFILLED

BY ANDREA TOWERS SCOTT

*D*ad was dying. I knew this, yet it was incomprehensible. Certainly, Dad was invincible. But life revealed the horrible truth. My sisters and I fervently prayed for him to turn to God and seek salvation before it was too late.

I was eighteen when two dear college friends brought me to the Lord. Despite growing up a "holiday Catholic," I didn't understand the message of salvation. These two sweet women shared the love of Christ with me, and my life has never been the same. Since then, I've embraced growing stronger in my faith.

My father, on the other hand, has been an atheist his whole life. Despite my sisters and I praying for him over the years, he remained steadfast in his unbelief.

Ten years ago, he developed vascular dementia. When he began to show more overt signs of dementia, he told my eldest sister that he would attend church with her. Given his declining mental state, we were never sure he really understood what he heard. But we knew the Word was sinking into his spirit either way. And he did enjoy the music.

Dad also regularly walked with a godly man from down the

street. We knew the man was a Christian and we held out hope that he would tell dad about the love of Jesus.

Toward the end of his life, his walking partner and the pastor from the church he occasionally attended went to see him. We had no idea what they said, but there was no evidence that Dad accepted Christ.

Dad passed on October 28, 2022. We mourned the loss of our father and the fact that he never knew Christ before passing. Saddened by our prayers not being answered, we helped Mom make funeral arrangements.

One of the speakers at the funeral was Dad's walking buddy. The man said that he brought up topics of faith but never took the time to actually share the Good News with Dad. Tearfully, he asked our forgiveness for not ensuring that Dad knew Christ. We were moved yet heartbroken that he was not able to take the leap to share Christ with our father.

The next speaker was the pastor from the church Dad occasionally attended with my sister. He recalled seeing Dad in church over the last year and getting to know him better toward the end of his life with home visits. He thanked the walking friend for spending time with Dad and planting seeds of faith.

With a big smile, the pastor said, "I'm thrilled to tell you ladies that your father accepted Christ on October 11, roughly two weeks before he went home to Jesus."

My spirit soared. Our persistent prayers were answered. This truly seemed like a miracle. For seventy-eight years, Dad was an atheist, but the message of hope and salvation was able to turn his heart to Christ. Now my sisters and I can live with joyful anticipation for the day we will see him again.

* * *

Andrea Towers Scott is an author, speaker, and professor. Her passion is helping women to build a family that thrives in Christ.

Andrea has been married to a wonderful man for thirty years and they have two sons—a young adult and a teen. You can find Andrea at www.DrAndreaTowersScott.com.

Questions for Personal Reflection or Group Discussion

Andrea and her sisters prayed for many years for their father, an atheist, to accept Christ. Even in the face of his declining mental health, they held onto hope. Just two weeks before his death, their father accepted Jesus, a testament to the power of persistent prayer and God's ability to work miracles even at the end of life.

1. How do you stay hopeful when it feels like your prayers aren't being answered right away?
2. Have you ever experienced a situation where God answered a long-awaited prayer in an unexpected or miraculous way?
3. How does this story encourage you to continue praying for loved ones who don't yet know Christ?

We pray that Andrea's story will remind you that God hears every prayer, even when the answers take time. May it inspire you to keep praying for your loved ones, trusting that God is always at work, even when we cannot see it. Let this testimony give you hope that it's never too late for someone to come to faith, and that God's timing is always perfect.

ANGEL OVER AFGHANISTAN

BY M. ANN JOLISSAINT

*I*n 2009, our son deployed to Afghanistan with his Army National Guard unit. My husband and I had many concerns, and thoughts of the unknown were too overwhelming because of the very nature of war. Nevertheless, we tried not to fret or worry, but to trust God to lead and protect him.

Time went by, and one day, our son called from Afghanistan. Today's technology is so amazing, allowing us to communicate with our son through cell phone across the world as though he were in the same room with us. Tyler's voice was intense, and fear shouted out of his mouth.

He said, "Mom and Dad, *pray, pray, pray.* I am on a suicide mission." Those words were very frightening to hear as we realized there was nothing we could do physically to help.

As it turned out, the mission he and four other soldiers were commissioned to do was to be helicoptered out and dropped into a town in Afghanistan to help the Afghan police secure the area. Taliban soldiers surrounded the town.

As you can imagine, my husband and I began praying, and we

contacted our church to pray as well. That night, as I was about to go to bed, I heard the voice of the Holy Spirit: *"Pray that Tyler becomes invisible to the enemy."* I shared this with my husband, and we prayed together. We covered our son, praying Psalm 91 and committing our fears and worries to God, trusting that He would watch over him with His holy protection.

During the mission, Tyler and the other four men from his unit were on the roof of the police station with mortar rounds going overhead. It was seriously intense with the sounds of war all around them.

Suddenly, Tyler saw a bright light in the sky and asked everyone around him, including the Afghan policemen, what the bright light in the sky was. No one had ever seen the light before, and no one could explain it.

Tyler said later that when he saw the light in the sky, peace penetrated through his body from his head to his feet. At that moment, he knew it was his guardian angel watching over him. He said, after his duty watch was over, that it was so peaceful that he fell asleep on top of that police station. As long as the bright light stayed in the sky above him, there was no sound of war.

We know in our hearts that, that day in Afghanistan, when our son was on top of the police station, God heard our prayers and sent an angel to guard and protect him as though he were invisible. Not only was our son saved that day, but all those who were with him that day were also saved.

We later found out our church prayer warriors prayed the same thing the Holy Spirit had told my husband and me to pray: *"Pray that Tyler becomes invisible to the enemy."*

"He will shield you with His wings. He will shelter you with His feathers ... . For He orders His angels to protect you wherever you go" (Psalm 91:4a, 11).

Without a shadow of a doubt, we will always be grateful and thankful as we give God glory and honor. His amazing grace shielded our son that day in his hour of need, and He sent an angel over Afghanistan to guard and protect him from war. God truly answers prayer!

* * *

M. Ann Jolissaint is a retired military wife, mother, and grandmother. She enjoys Christian writing, has been featured in *The Upper Room*, and is the author of *Refining Times.* Ann is passionate about her nine grandchildren and enjoys Cajun cooking, biking, and vacationing at the lake.

Questions for Personal Reflection or Group Discussion

Ann and her husband faced the terrifying reality of their son being sent on a dangerous mission in Afghanistan. Despite their fear, they turned to prayer, asking God for divine protection. In response to their prayers and those of their church, God sent a miraculous sign: a bright light that brought peace to their son and protected him from the enemy.

1. How does Ann's story encourage you to trust God's protection, even when you feel powerless to help a loved one in danger?
2. Have you ever experienced a moment when prayer brought peace in the midst of fear or uncertainty?
3. How does this story inspire you to pray specifically and boldly, trusting that God hears and answers in miraculous ways?

We pray that Ann's story will remind you of God's powerful protection and His ability to send help in even the most dangerous situations. May it encourage you to trust in the promises of Psalm 91 and to pray for God's intervention when you or your loved ones are in need. Let this testimony strengthen your faith in God's ability to protect and deliver, no matter the circumstances.

THE COMMANDER OF GOD'S ARMY

BY DIANE W. BAILEY

"*A*re you alright?" I smile and nod. My husband, Doc, winks at me as my son, Jake, extends his arm to his new bride.

I whispered a prayer of thanks, for the millionth time, for the miracle I am witnessing.

Three years earlier...

"Ma'am, are you alright?" asked a nurse.

I had fled from the side of my son into the hall as my stomach lurched and cold beads of sweat lined my upper lip.

"I think so," I choked out as emotions became clogged in my throat.

"I didn't know ... I had never seen ... ." I couldn't say any more.

Inhale slowly ...

Exhale slowly ...

Swallow hard ...

Hand on the hospital room door ...

I willed myself to return to his side.

They laid my son's arm on the bed. Then, the nurses decided to start an IV in his leg as all the veins in his arms were scared and collapsed from street drug injections.

Earlier that morning, before daylight, Jake called me to ask why I was talking outside his window.

"Son, I'm still in bed in my house."

This was not the first call of this kind from him the past few months. Street drugs can induce hallucinations, paranoia, and voices that are inaudible to others but very real to the addict.

"Mom, I think I need to go to the hospital."

"I am on the way. Stay on the phone with me, baby."

No matter how old they are, they are still your baby.

No matter how old they are, when they cry out in the night for you, you run to them as quickly as possible.

"Stay on the phone with me!"

I had prayed for this child for years. Illegal drugs had become his escape from memories of an unkind childhood at the hands of someone who should have been his shield and defender.

Doc drove me to Jake's house as I kept him talking on the phone.

"I think he has overdosed," I mouth to Doc. His face grimaces and with a slow nod, he presses down on the gas pedal.

Speeding down the streets at 3:00 AM, streetlights ebb and fade as I try to think of questions to keep the right and left side of Jake's brain active. At the same time, I am sending urgent text messages asking for urgent prayer.

"Can you tell me your street address?"

"Sing to me your favorite song."

"What is your phone number?"

"Where do you want to go on vacation?"

"Can you say the Pledge of Allegiance?"

Between each question, he engages in a conversation with someone who is not there, then he returns to me with answers to my questions.

For years I had prayed for God to heal Jake's addiction. It tortured me as I watched him sink deeper into drugs. I was desperate enough to tell God that if He would not heal him on this side of Heaven, then maybe He should call him Home to keep him safe.

When he was younger, he would tell anyone who would listen about God's love. I never would have dreamed that this tenderhearted one would be dragged down this dark and evil path of drugs.

The doctors came in to suggest drug rehab. Gently touching my son's needle-scarred arm, I agreed.

Jake awakened.

"Mom, I hear people talking that I cannot see. One of them wants you to know something. His name is Commander. When he speaks, all the other voices stop talking and obey him. He said to tell you that it's going to be okay."

"I am the commander of the army of the Lord. Now I have come."
Joshua 5:14

* * *

Diane W. Bailey has authored two books and been a contributor in many devotionals including Lifeway's devotional *A Moment to Breathe*. She and her husband live on Dragonfly Pond in the Deep South. She enjoys crafting jewelry, photography, and discovering deep places of the heart with Jesus.

Questions for Personal Reflection or Group Discussion

Diane's heart broke as she watched her son, Jake, battle drug addiction and experience its devastating effects. Despite her years of prayer and hope for healing, Jake continued down a dark path. But during one terrifying night, a miraculous message of hope came through Jake—God's commander reassured her that everything would be okay, bringing comfort and peace in the midst of the storm.

1. How does Diane's story encourage you to keep praying for loved ones, even when the situation seems hopeless?
2. Have you ever experienced a moment where God spoke peace to you in a desperate or fearful situation?
3. How can this story inspire you to trust in God's timing and His promises, even when the answers seem delayed?

We pray that Diane's story will remind you of God's faithfulness, even in life's most difficult moments. May it encourage you to continue praying for those who are struggling, trusting that God is always working behind the scenes. Let this testimony inspire you to hold on to hope, knowing that God's army is fighting for you and your loved ones, and His promises never fail.

THE ETERNAL VS. THE TEMPORARY

BY SUSAN KING

*A*s I walked into the empty chapel, the late afternoon sun had begun to pour through the stained-glass windows, spreading rainbow colors throughout room. The old diamond pattern made me think of old European churches.

Pushing through my workday, I was robotic, numb, eyes swollen from tears of sorrow. How could this be my life? It wasn't mine, but a stranger's. A year and a half earlier, I was a wife and mother who was walking forward with a sincere Christian heart, wanting a career in helping others.

I sat with a thud on the padded church pew, sobbing, and began to talk to God, asking the proverbial, *Why?* I had no idea how long I had been there, but there came a moment when I forced myself to take a hard look at all of the horrendous choices I had made in the last year that had me wallowing in a deep, carbon-black hole of sin. There was no one to blame but myself.

There was a cavern in my soul which began in my childhood, and it seemed bottomless. A relentless need for love, attention, even romance—I considered these needs life sustaining and felt I had lived without them my entire life.

In my nineteenth year of marriage, this hunger exploded into relational addiction. Where I was once invisible to the opposite sex, I was now getting attention because I had lost 150 pounds, believing it would bring me what I never had.

He was twelve years my junior, a talented musician, and an alcoholic. There are no words to describe the level of toxicity in this relationship. It was a nightmare that culminated in his cheating while I was out of town for my sister's funeral.

As I continued to sit in the chapel praying, suddenly it was as if God had flipped a switch in my mind. My words began to cry out not for myself, but for this man who had just torn my heart in two. I distinctly heard God instruct me, because of the man's musical talents, to write a song lyric for him. God instructed, *I want you to write this from the prospective of a broken-hearted Father.* Instantly, He took my focus from the temporary pain to the internal. I was obedient and wrote:

> *I see you lost out in the desert*
> *In heat too hard to bear*
> *Your soul lies bleeding open in the sand*
> *And as the years go by*
> *Your childhood memories die*
> *Of how your loving Father held your hand*
> *Where is my boy?*
> *My fair-haired gentle child?*
> *My precious blue-eyed son*
> *With music in his hands*
> *I've never let you go*
> *But what I need to know*
> *When will you call to me and when will you come home?*
> *I feel the longing of your heart*
> *I see the hunger in your eyes*
> *To run to me*
> *Surrender all your pain*
> *And through these many years*

I caught each tender tear
Each drop that fell into my hands
Like pouring rain
I've held on tight to you
And waited long nights through
For you to come to me
To hear you speak my name......

The choices he was making—that we were both making—were breaking the heart of God. I delivered this message to him, from what I believed, and will always believe, was the heart of God. In my brokenness and sorrow, I could have never written this without the touch of God on my soul. Yes, even in my sin, He loved me.

* * *

Susan King is a published author who embraces her gift of transparency, believing the honest sharing of the human experience, coupled with relationship with God, can impart healing to others.

Questions for Personal Reflection or Group Discussion

Susan shares her deeply personal story of grappling with the consequences of relational addiction and sin. While brokenhearted in a toxic relationship, she sought answers in prayer. In her lowest moment, God shifted her focus from temporary pain to an eternal perspective, inspiring her to write a song from the perspective of a loving Father, yearning for His child to return. This story highlights the tension between earthly desires and God's eternal love, as well as the transformative power of prayer, even in the midst of personal failure.

1. How does Susan's experience of God's forgiveness and guidance, even in her darkest moment, inspire you to turn to God for healing and direction, regardless of your situation?
2. Have you ever experienced a time when God shifted your perspective from focusing on the temporary to seeing things through His eternal lens? How did it change your outlook?
3. What can you learn from Susan's obedience in following God's instruction to write the song, even when she was struggling with her own pain and brokenness?

We pray that Susan's story reminds you that God's love is constant, even in our sin and mistakes. His heart breaks for us when we stray, but He is always ready to draw us back to Him, offering healing and a renewed sense of purpose.

39

THE FINGERTIP TOUCH

BY MELISSA HENDERSON

This is not happening to me.

A breast cancer diagnosis in 2005 brought emotions ranging from fear and sadness to anger and defiance. My father had passed from lung cancer in 1998, and my mother had dealt with breast cancer a few years before my diagnosis. The radiologist said, "We love your family, but please don't bring us more patients."

Treatment for my condition was surgery, radiation, chemotherapy, medications to be taken for about five years, and then many trips to the doctor's office for follow-up visits. At one of those appointments, the surgeon shared that another spot had been revealed on the most recent mammogram. I kept thinking, *Not again.*

The surgeon scheduled a breast MRI. That was trouble because I was extremely claustrophobic. I tried to figure a way out of that dreaded test in the tube-like tunnel. The doctor reassured me that I would be fine. The MRI would not take long, and she could prescribe medicine to relax my body. As I pleaded for another way to scan the area of concern, my sweet doctor gathered my hands in hers and said, "We have to do this test."

My sister Glenda had driven me to this appointment. She knew of my fears and reassured me that she would not leave the waiting room. I was comforted by her presence but could not calm my nerves. I asked the surgeon if my sister could be in the room. Normally, no one is allowed in the area of the big machine. The radiologists wear protective gear and step into a small cubicle to proceed with the scan.

I prayed and asked God to help me know what to do with my fear. Scriptures filled my thoughts. Prayers for protection, calm, peace, and a quick procedure were not enough to ease my fears. Or, at least, that is what I thought. God was working His plan.

The surgeon spoke to the radiologist. After their conversation, the decision was made. Since this was an MRI on one breast, I would be lying on my stomach with one arm stretched out. My other arm would be positioned directly by my side. My sister was allowed to sit in a chair and touch my fingertips during the test. She agreed to help.

Positioned on the table, my eyes were closed. I prayed that I had not dreamed or misunderstood that my sister would be close by. Asking God to guide me to feel His presence, I lay still and waited. A voice came on the intercom in the room and alerted me that the MRI was about to begin.

God filled me with His peace. I was not alone. God was there, and my sister was there too. The procedure was completed in a few minutes. My anxiety left the moment I felt the fingertip touch of my sister.

My prayers were answered. The results of the test were good. God listened and heard my cries. He placed my sister, surgeon, radiologist, and other people in the exact places they needed to be so that I would be comforted. I praise God for His love.

* * *

Award-winning author **Melissa Henderson** writes inspirational messages sometimes humming with humor. Melissa is the author of *Licky the Lizard* and *Grumpy the Gator*. Melissa is an elder, deacon and Stephen Minister. Follow Melissa on Facebook, Twitter, Pinterest, Instagram, Goodreads, Bookbub, YouTube, LinkedIn, and at http://www.melissaghenderson.com.

Questions for Personal Reflection or Group Discussion

Melissa faced the fear and uncertainty of a breast cancer diagnosis followed by a difficult MRI test due to her claustrophobia. In her moment of anxiety, God provided comfort through her sister's presence and touch, helping her endure the procedure with peace. The test results were positive, reminding Melissa that God hears and answers prayers, even in the most fearful situations.

1. How does Melissa's story encourage you to trust in God's presence and peace during times of fear or anxiety?
2. Have you ever experienced a moment when God provided comfort through the presence or actions of a loved one?
3. How can this story inspire you to turn to God in prayer, trusting that He will place the right people in your life to support you through difficult circumstances?

We pray that Melissa's story will remind you of God's ability to bring peace and comfort in moments of fear and uncertainty. May it encourage you to trust in His presence, knowing that He listens to your prayers and works through the people around you to bring you the support and peace you need. Let this testimony inspire you to rely on God's guidance, trusting that He is with you in every situation, no matter how daunting it may seem.

40

FINDING GOD'S PEACE

BY DAWN KENNEDY

*P*eace. I used to think that I had peace and would always have it. After all, I know the Lord Jesus as my Savior, the One who is abiding with me every day.

Then, one day during a routine medical visit, the doctor requested a CT scan for an area of concern. Although the radiologist posted his report for the doctor, I too was able to view it on my patient portal. Not wanting to wait to hear the results from my doctor, I read the report. Then like so many others, I immediately went straight to the trusty Internet.

Fear started to rise up within me while reading about the many possibilities it could be. I knew I should have waited until I heard from the doctor, but I couldn't resist the temptation to seek the answers. The more I read, the more confused I became. I wanted to know it was all going to be fine, that I was not dying. That once confident peace was now gone.

Questions and thoughts consumed me as I went through the many tests and procedures that followed. Things like, *Are the doctors evaluating everything? Are they missing something? Why is what they are telling me or not telling me not lining up with what I was finding on the Internet?*

Finally, my daughter, who is a nurse, got very direct with me. She told me to stay off the Internet! The Internet does not know me on a personal level. It does not have all my tests in front of it. It is not my doctor who has known me for many years. I have to trust your doctor, not the Internet.

I did listen to her, but I was still drowning in the fear of the unknown.

Why did I have this fear of the unknown if I know and trust Jesus Christ? Paul wrote in Philippians 4:7, "And the peace of God, which surpasses all comprehension will guard your hearts and your minds in Christ Jesus." Shouldn't I have this kind of peace that surpasses all comprehension? But I didn't. Fear was consuming me. The lump in my throat, the shaking hands, and the anxiety taking over my body—they were uncontrollable. Peace was not found.

While I knew I should trust in the One who knows my tomorrows, I didn't. I tried to pray and asked my friends to pray. I had thoughts of a million reasons why God was not hearing me. Nothing was giving me peace. The psalmist wrote in Psalms 145:18, "The Lord is near to all who call on Him, to all who call on Him in truth." So, being at my wits end, I dropped to my knees beside the bed. I cried out to the Lord, surrendering my fears to Him, begging for His peace. Somehow releasing it all to Him was like releasing the world off my shoulders.

As the days passed, it became evident that no matter how hard I tried to worry, I could not. All through each of the processes to find answers to my problem, I was unable to worry! I finally had complete peace. I now understood what it is like to have the peace that surpasses all comprehension. God did not abandon me, but instead heard and answered my prayer. Oh, what joy and comfort to have His love and peace fill my soul!

* * *

Dawn Kennedy has been serving the Lord in women's ministry for thirty years. She has written devotions for several years in her Facebook group called "Encouraging Women in God's Word." She hopes that through her writing, women will be encouraged and grow in their walk with the Lord.

Questions for Personal Reflection or Group Discussion

Dawn's peace was shattered when she let fear and worry over a medical concern consume her, seeking answers online instead of trusting in God. It wasn't until she surrendered her fears in prayer that she found the peace she had been missing. Through this experience, Dawn came to understand the kind of peace that surpasses all understanding, which only God can give.

1. Have you ever let fear and worry overtake you when facing the unknown? How did it affect your sense of peace?
2. How can you learn to trust God in times of uncertainty rather than relying on your own understanding or external sources?
3. How does Dawn's story encourage you to bring your fears to God in prayer, trusting that He will give you peace?

We pray that Dawn's story will remind you of the peace that only God can provide, even in life's most uncertain moments. May it inspire you to trust in God's plan and surrender your worries to Him, knowing that He hears your prayers and will give you the peace that surpasses all comprehension. Let this testimony encourage you to lean on God's promises and experience His peace in every circumstance.

41

AT DEATH'S DOOR

BY ELNA EAYRS

*T*he midday winter sun warms my skin. The wind is chilly, but I love this time in silence with You, Lord. The sheep and ostriches eye the bags of vegetables in my hand, but I am lost in my thoughts ...

"Hubby, please phone Mom; I can't anymore." Those were my words—a cry of desperation. *Lord, why? I knew You said I would go through this, but why me, Lord?*

It was the early hours of May 27, 2021. The Delta variant of COVID-19 had hit South Africa hard. My oxygen levels were dropping severely, dipping below seventy percent. Breathing was becoming more and more difficult. Hubby called Mom, and with her help and our last savings, I was admitted to the hospital at two o'clock in the morning.

God's warning became a reality. I could still hear a mother crying, "Please don't give up. Fight, fight, increase your oxygen levels." This unknown mother cried out to God with such intensity. I was drifting in and out of consciousness. I didn't know what day it was, but I realized it was Mom's birthday. Summoning my last bit of strength, I grabbed the phone, short of breath, and congratulated her.

I remember phoning Hubby, telling him that Satan was attacking me. I saw a black figure peering around the door into my bedroom. In my subconscious, the only thing I knew to do was plead the Blood of Jesus over me. This became a daily struggle. I had dreams of Satan telling me I had three chances left. Each time, I saw all the nurses surrounding me, with Satan grinning at the back. Then, the nurse would wake me, asking why I was screaming that I was suffocating. She checked my oxygen level, and it was at ninety-seven percent. This happened a second time, but then it stopped.

It was June 8, my son's birthday. The nurse snuck Hubby in for a two-minute visit. Nothing more, but I was on the road to recovery. Four days later, I was released from the hospital.

The ostrich pecking at the bag brings me back to reality. I start tossing off-cut vegetables to them. As I sit down, watching them, my thoughts drift again.

How great You are, Lord! Hubby created a WhatsApp group and a GoFundMe to cover the costs. People were praying for me. *You heard their prayers. My father-in-law and Mom both testified that You reassured them I would be okay.*

Here I am today, Lord, with a thankful heart. Thank You for clearing the $10,000 medical bill so quickly. Thank You for the financial help we received while I was recovering. Thank You for the job You provided for me when Hubby lost his—a job beyond my wildest dreams.

Lord, today I pray that Pippa will also get that job. You know how much she wants to teach online after just graduating.

The ringing of my smartwatch snaps me back to reality. It's Pippa.

"Yes, dear," I say, holding back tears.

"Mom, I got the job."

"I'm overjoyed, Pips! Yes, I'm on my way home now."

I start heading home, leaving the bags of vegetables behind at the fence. As I leave the park, the Lord's voice echoes in my soul:

The Lord is listening! Joy and gratitude flood my heart. I come to a halt, realizing that God still has a plan for me. As I stroll home, God gently reminds me, *Be still, and know that I am God. I AM.*

* * *

Elna Eayrs is co-pastor with her husband, Edward Eayrs, at Spontaan Ministries in South Africa. She also owns her own tutoring company, WestmeadowEdu, and is a financial literacy teacher. She has a podcast, Westmeadowmom, and has written articles for homeschool magazines. Elna is a ghostwriter, and her favorite pastime is spending time with her dogs and family.

Questions for Personal Reflection or Group Discussion

In the midst of a terrifying battle with COVID-19, Elna clung to her faith, even as she struggled with visions of darkness and despair. Despite the overwhelming circumstances, she experienced God's protection, healing, and provision through the power of prayer and the support of her family. As she reflects on her miraculous recovery and the blessings that followed, she is filled with gratitude for God's faithfulness.

1. How do you respond when life feels overwhelming, and you can't see a way out?
2. Have you ever experienced God's protection in a moment of fear or despair? How did it change your faith?
3. How does this story encourage you to remain still and trust in God's presence, even in difficult times?

We pray that Elna's story will remind you of the power of prayer and God's presence, even in the darkest moments. May it encourage you to trust in His plan for your life, knowing that He hears your prayers and is always working behind the scenes. Let this testimony inspire you to hold on to faith, no matter how difficult the road may seem, and to give thanks for the ways God works miracles, both big and small.

MY BROTHER RETURNS TO CHRIST

BY TODD KNOWLES

*M*y older brother, Barry, was being treated for cancer, and our family was struggling with how to pray. In 2013, he had a portion of his colon removed at only fifty-five years old. Barry's son, Colin, arrived from out of town to help him through all of his treatment. While everyone in my family of origin developed cancer, Barry's cancer was more severe. Further, there was an additional dynamic requiring urgent prayer in Barry's case. Let me explain.

In the mid-1970s, Barry began learning to play the guitar. He listened to numerous musicians and vocalists, attempting to imitate their style on his journey to becoming a highly proficient musician. Although Dad and Mom encouraged him, something changed for Barry, a change which became quite difficult for the family. Barry's friends were also musicians, but they did not attend church. Additionally, one of Barry's high school teachers taught about evolution and that there was no God. This was quite different from what Barry was used to hearing.

Eventually, Barry talked with Dad and Mom about his new desire to skip church, wanting instead to practice music with his friends. I remember the conversation well, as we were all outside on the patio; the three talked while I performed chores. Dad and Mom were trying to see Barry's point of view, yet they desired Barry to know the Savior and be in church fellowship. They agonized in their prayers for God to work in his heart. Eventually, they allowed Barry to refrain from attending church.

Dad and Mom had chosen to be gentle as they raised all of us, far differently than what they experienced in their own youth. Mom was beaten by her grandfather whenever she showed emotion, and he would tell her she would never amount to anything. Dad's mom had been an orphan and was raised by foster parents. Her foster mother was so abusive that she developed tremendous emotional pain that she took out on my dad. While his older brother, Connie, could do no wrong in my grandmother's eyes, Dad would frequently be ignored as if he weren't important to his mom and was punished even for things he thought he accomplished well.

My parents purposely chose to keep such hostility and abuse out of our home and instead be as supportive as possible. Consequently, they believed that by granting Barry leeway, they would provide a home where he always felt welcome. They hoped this would leave a door open, helping Barry one day to have a clear path back to the Lord.

During the next several years, without allowing God in his life, Barry experienced further negative influence from his friends, leading to him spending several months in a youth detention center after driving the getaway car in a store holdup. In Barry's thirties and forties, he married and was divorced three times, eventually telling us he felt like God hated him.

When he was diagnosed with colon cancer, Barry's feelings about God may have been reinforced. My parents, my sister, and I struggled in our prayers both for his spiritual and physical needs. Throughout Barry's life, we asked God to use any situation to make Himself known to him, but God respects a person's free will. Finally, we realized that even while we wanted his physical healing, Barry's biggest need was Jesus. We asked the Holy Spirit to use the cancer to open Barry's heart and show him his need. Finally, as Barry lay dying, my nephew Colin told us that Barry cried out to Jesus. In those last moments, Barry saw his need and chose his Savior once again.

* * *

Todd Knowles spent almost thirty-seven years with the Department of the Air Force on active duty and as a civilian employee. Twenty-eight of those years were spent as an educator. Todd is retired and lives in Montgomery, Alabama, with his wonderful wife, Heather. They have four grown children and five grandchildren.

Questions for Personal Reflection or Group Discussion

Todd's heartfelt account of his brother Barry's return to Jesus is an important reminder of the power of prayer, even when it seems like hope is lost. Diagnosed with colon cancer at fifty-five, Barry's battle was compounded by years of estrangement from God. His family, particularly his parents, had long prayed for him, hoping for both his physical recovery and spiritual restoration. In his final moments, Barry's heart softened, and he cried out to Jesus. This story reminds us that while physical healing is important, the greatest need is always for spiritual salvation.

1. How does Barry's story encourage you to continue praying for loved ones who may have turned away from their faith?
2. What does this story teach us about the role of free will and God's grace in someone's spiritual journey?
3. How can Todd's experience inspire you to trust in God's

timing and plan, even in difficult or seemingly hopeless situations?

We pray that Todd's story will encourage you to keep praying for those you love, trusting that God is always working in their hearts, even when you can't see it. Let this testimony inspire you to have faith that no one is ever too far from God's grace and that His love reaches even into the final moments of life. God is always ready to welcome those who turn to Him, no matter how long it takes.

A WINDY DAY

BY JANE BECKER WEATHERS

*H*alfway down the coast of the Baja California peninsula, my son, Kent, his wife, Heidi, and their two sons, Dylan, aged six, and Connor, three, sailed on their fifty-two-foot ketch with the sun gleaming on its deck.

Kent and Heidi knew that "Buy a boat and sail" was on many bucket lists. These youngsters wanted to live their dream and not wait until old age disabled them. Their ketch came from one such dreamer, and they named their prize *Elandria*, which means "House by the Sea."

Kent and Heidi sailed from San Diego in early February with the goal of reaching Australia by Christmas. Their itinerary included some forty ports, and as they sailed down the Mexican coast, they anticipated reaching Turtle Bay in three and a half days.

My mental picture was a little boat on the ocean. I would pass eighteen wheelers, see 53' printed on the trailer behind the driver, and think, *That?* On the *Pacific Ocean?*

With confidence, Kent and Heidi followed maps and current condition reports. Family members had access to an Internet tracking device, displaying the pathway and the hourly location of *Elandria*.

It was Wednesday, and their hope was to reach Turtle Bay that evening. From over a thousand miles away, I watched until bedtime.

Early Thursday morning, I was astounded to see *Elandria's* location the same as the night before, even having retraced a little of the route. Kent and Heidi had sailed small distances, but nothing of this magnitude. An early morning email was unanswered.

I rushed to get ready for our JOY Community Choir, performing at a rest home. The mood was joyous, but concern for my sailors surfaced many times. Prayers for safety were breathed between songs and phrases. Our repertoire included "Just a Little Talk with Jesus Makes It Right" and "So let the storms rage high, the dark clouds rise, they won't worry me, for I'm sheltered safe within the arms of God." My songs were prayers for the sailors, and God's comfort for me.

By early afternoon, the dot in the ocean still had not moved. "Could we beg the San Diego Coast Guard to check on *Elandria*?" I queried.

"And they would answer a call from mid-America?" was my husband's retort.

Time seemed to move slowly. My phone text was not answered. Prayers were breathed, but my fingers began to quiver and tremble on the table. God's letter came into view. I opened it and read, "Therefore I tell you, whatever you ask for in prayer, believe that you have received it and it will be yours." Trust replaced worry as I thought of our sovereign God, watching a tiny boat on a huge ocean. With a finger, He could swish *Elandria* to safety. Amazingly, my faith, like an anchor, gave me hope and held me in peace. I could sing, "It is well with my soul." It was like safety near a lighthouse.

Early that evening, Heidi's email arrived: "We encountered

some forty-knot winds near Turtle Bay, so we turned around and came back to Cedros Island. We are now safely moored and will be here until Monday as the port is closed due to high seas. Everybody is doing well."

During the storm, the tracking device had been taken below deck, out of the rain, out of service and view.

The friendly people of Cedros Island assisted *Elandria's* crew after a windy day. My praises arose in thanks, smiles, and songs to my precious, caring Lord in Heaven.

* * *

Jane Becker Weathers studied at John Brown University and taught for twenty-four years. Her passion for the Bible led her to develop *Chronological Bible Reading Guide,* which incorporates literature with history. She lives with her husband in Siloam Springs, Arkansas. For more information, see www.ChronoBibleGuide.com.

Questions for Personal Reflection or Group Discussion

As Kent and Heidi faced treacherous winds while sailing with their young sons, their family anxiously followed their journey from afar, praying for their safety. Although worry threatened to take hold, faith and prayer became a source of strength and peace. In the end, God answered those prayers, guiding the family safely to Cedros Island.

1. How do you handle worry or fear when someone you love is in danger?
2. Have you ever experienced a time when God's peace replaced your anxiety? How did it impact your faith?
3. How does this story encourage you to trust in God's

protection and provision, even when you cannot see the outcome?

We pray that Jane's story will inspire you to lean on God during moments of uncertainty, and to trust that He is always watching over your loved ones. May it remind you of the power of prayer and the peace that comes from believing in God's sovereignty, particularly when the circumstances seem overwhelming. Let this testimony encourage you to pray with confidence, knowing that God holds us securely, even in life's storms.

44

JESUS SAVED MY LIFE

BY TINA WHITE

I remember that my van had gone airborne. I could see dirt flying on the window shield, and I heard glass breaking. All I could do was cry out, "Jesus take the wheel!"

In the years prior to this accident, I experienced symptoms of excessive daytime drowsiness. I would have a super difficult time staying awake during the day. I would repeatedly fall asleep numerous times a day. I could and would fall asleep while cooking, taking a walk, watching TV, driving, and even showering. Even though I would have a good night's sleep, I would still have trouble staying awake. This was starting to take its toll on my life. Plus, I didn't realize the severity of the possible consequences it could have.

One spring afternoon, I had gone to see my family physician for an appointment. Her office was only about twenty minutes from where I was living at the time. As I was driving back home from that appointment, the excessive daytime drowsiness began to kick in, and I could feel myself dozing off at the wheel. I kept forcing myself to wake up, reminding myself that I was only five minutes from my house. *I can make it safely home*, I thought.

Within those five minutes, though, I fell asleep again, and my minivan began to swerve off the road. As the van swerved, it hit the corner of a ditch, rolled five times, and then hit an electric pole before finally coming to a stop.

In the traffic report, the drivers of the cars behind me who witnessed the accident said that my van hit the corner of the ditch and electric pole so hard that impacts tore off the hood of the van. Parts of the motor broke off and were lying on the ground.

All the windows were shattered, and three of the tires were flat. The drivers who were behind me had stopped and run to my van to check on me. A man who owned the property where my van came to a rest grabbed a crowbar and pried open the driver's door so I could get out. They all thought I'd be dead or badly injured because of the severity of the accident they had witnessed.

But praise be to the Lord, I didn't have even a scratch on me. Physically, I was completely fine. Yes, I was extremely shaken up, but other than that, and the fact that my van was totaled, I walked away from that accident knowing it was the God I serve who had His hands on me that day.

My symptoms were consistent with narcolepsy, the hospital said, and I was diagnosed with the condition two weeks later. I also surrendered my driver's license.

I strongly believe that in that very second, when I woke up as the van was rolling and yelled, "Jesus, take the wheel!" that Jesus *did* take the wheel. He spared my life that day, and He also protected all the other drivers on the road.

Due to the severity of the accident, I should not have survived that day. Or, at the very least, I should have suffered severe injuries. I know it was God who protected me. The enemy tried to snatch me that day, but God said, *No, I have a plan for her.*

"For I know the plans I have for you," declares the Lord, "plans to prosper you and not to harm you, plans to give you hope and a future."
Jeremiah 29:11

* * *

Tina White is a daughter, sister, aunt, great-aunt, godmother, chaplain, and author. She has published two books, *Renewed Gem: A Daughter of the King* and *Think on These Things: Self-Empowerment Prompts Journal for Christians*, both by Queen Tamar and available on Amazon. She has also published two short stories.

Questions for Personal Reflection or Group Discussion

Tina experienced a life-threatening car accident when she fell asleep at the wheel due to undiagnosed narcolepsy. As her van rolled, she cried out for Jesus to take control, and miraculously, she survived without a scratch. Tina's story is a powerful reminder of God's protection and His plans for her life.

1. How does Tina's story encourage you to trust God in moments of crisis or danger?
2. Have you ever experienced a time when you called on Jesus in a desperate situation? How did He respond?
3. How does Tina's story remind you of God's purpose and plan for your life, even when things seem out of control?

We pray that Tina's story will remind you of the power of calling on Jesus in times of need. May it encourage you to trust in His protection and believe that God has a purpose for your life, no matter the challenges you face. Let this testimony inspire you to lean on God's strength and to remember that He is always in control, guiding and protecting you even in the most difficult circumstances.

45

THE FIVE-MINUTE PASTOR

BY JULIE CROTTY-GUILE

I felt like a clean and empty cistern after a thirty-minute meditation, during which I centered my mind and cleared it of all distracting thoughts. Afterwards, I took a long drive to the car wash. I often had good luck there, finding items in my car's black interior that I couldn't locate on my own due to my blind right eye. But something stopped me. I felt an inner tug, like a dolphin calling to a friend, urging me to call Lori. She answered the phone as she waited for her Friday night Al-Anon meeting to begin.

After her parting words, "Safe drive," I pressed the gas pedal like an ambulance driver responding to an emergency, and soon I arrived at Hosanna Lutheran Church, right on time.

As I entered the room, I heard ... nothing! Frustrated, embarrassed, and alone in a room full of friends, I touched my ears—I had forgotten my hearing aids.

Trying to keep my serenity, I walked out of the meeting and headed toward my Nissan. Suddenly, I heard a voice, caterwauling in broken English, "Where is the muck sur, pastor?"

A man with almond-shaped eyes and a slight hunch approached me. His voice dropped, and I couldn't hear him anymore. I beckoned him closer, slightly fearful. As we stood almost face-to-face, a warm, compassionate feeling hovered between us like a gentle breeze.

I asked him directly, "What is it you need?"

He showed me two videos on his iPhone. The first broke my heart—it was of his older brother, whom he said had terminal cancer and had taken his own life. The second video showed a group trying to raise money to bury his brother. Without judgment or hesitation, I felt the Holy Spirit guide me, and I placed my arm around this strange, seemingly unattractive little man. Words I didn't expect spilled from my mouth: "There's nobody at the church right now. I will be your pastor."

The story of the poor widow flashed across my mind as I moved toward my car. Once inside, I found fourteen twenty-dollar bills in my wallet. I knew God had provided this in advance. I left two dollars in case of an emergency.

I carefully took the money and placed the folded bills into Nan's small hands. I told him my name and said, "I believe in Jesus Christ!" Immediately, he bowed deeply and reverently. I bowed back.

The freedom of giving nearly everything I had at that moment created even more trust in God in the days that followed, and many of my financial worries lessened as I grew in my love for the Lord and His grace. I found myself with more time to meet Jesus in daily prayer. Of course, something inside questioned whether I had done enough for this man. After all, I could've invited him to our prayer group later that month. I continued to pray for Nan.

Secondly, I wasn't sure if I should share this good deed with anyone, though I did tell my husband and Lori, hoping it would strengthen their faith.

In the bigger picture, I learned once again the value of sacrifice and generosity as vital ways to please the Lord. Sometimes, we ordinary people are the only ones to do God's work in a desperate time of need.

* * *

Julie Crotty-Guile is a thirty-six-year-sober deaf and partially blind woman who has written poetry and songs since age twelve. She has been married thirty-five years to an Australian gentleman with two dependents. Julie is on peritoneal dialysis nightly as she waits for a healthy kidney donor. She plays piano for church, teaches piano and voice, and performs.

Questions for Personal Reflection or Group Discussion

In this heartfelt encounter, Julie feels compelled to help a stranger named Nan who is grieving his brother's death. Led by the Holy Spirit, she offers him comfort, prayer, and nearly all the money she has with her, trusting in God's provision. Reflecting on the experience, Julie finds reassurance in her faith, recognizing that sometimes God places us in situations where we are the only ones who can help.

1. How can you recognize when the Holy Spirit is prompting you to take action?
2. Have you ever felt uncertain about whether you did enough to help someone? How did you handle it?
3. What sacrifices are you willing to make to meet the needs of others, and how does this deepen your faith?

We pray that Julie's story will remind you to trust in God's guidance, even in unexpected moments. When we give of ourselves, especially in times of sacrifice, we reflect God's love and grace. Let this story encourage you to be bold in following the Holy Spirit's lead, knowing that God equips you to be a light for others in their time of need.

46

A DAUGHTER'S VIGIL

BY LENORA E. TREMBATH

*T*he jingling of my keys pierced the night air as I reached for the front door. Before I could turn the lock, it swung open, revealing Mom's pale face, her eyes rimmed with red.

"Get ready," she whispered, her voice quivering. "I'll take you to see Dad. It's his heart. The doctor says he's got a twenty percent chance of surviving."

The world tilted beneath my feet. My fingers fumbled for my phone, dialing familiar numbers. "Please pray," I pleaded to three friends, my words tumbling out in a rush.

The car ride to Eden Hospital was a blur of streetlights and shadows. My silent prayer echoed in my mind: *God, please give me the assurance of my dad's salvation and a clear-thinking mind.* I understood God had to initiate the conversation so I'd know it was His timing, not mine.

Stepping into the ICU, I was engulfed by a disorienting flood of mechanical noises. The rhythmic *beep-beep-beep* of heart monitors mingled with the *hiss-click* of ventilators. I hesitated at the threshold of Dad's room, my knuckles white as I gripped the doorframe. The sight of him, dwarfed by machines and tangled in a web of tubes, made my breath catch in my throat.

Whir-click. Whir-click. The mechanical beat of the IV pump marked the passing seconds as I approached his bedside. With only two visitors allowed, I waited, my chest reverberating with anticipation. When my brother left, Dad's eyes immediately locked onto mine. He blurted, "When you go to the Holy Land, pray that I make it through those pearly gates." (I was taking this trip in a couple of weeks.)

My heart thundered. This was the moment I'd prayed for. "You're not sure if you'll make it through the pearly gates?" I asked, steadying my voice.

A half-remembered verse tumbled from my lips. "If you believe in the name of Jesus, you will enter into Heaven."

"I believe," his voice strong. "I believe!" Immediately after, my uncle walked in. The precious conversation was over.

Relief washed over me. In that sterile room, a miracle had occurred.

Hours later, at home, the shrill ring of the telephone shattered the pre-dawn silence. "Dad's taken a turn for the worse."

My older brother and I raced back to the hospital, but all the familiar ICU sounds were replaced with silence, broken only by the quiet sobs of my family.

In the days that followed, grief wrapped around me like a heavy blanket. But beneath the weight of sorrow, a small flame of comfort flickered. I clung to the memory of Dad's last words, replaying them like a lifeline.

I found a letter Dad had written me a couple of years earlier. As I read his words again, calling me "nicer than human but not quite an angel, because angels had wings," I could almost hear his voice, see his proud smile.

Tears blurred my vision, but they weren't entirely of sadness. God had answered my desperate prayer, granting me the assurance I needed in those final moments with Dad.

The pain of loss still ached, but mixed with it now was a bittersweet joy. Each memory of our time together became a treasure, carefully wrapped and stored in my heart.

I whispered a quiet *thank you*—for the father he'd become, for the love we'd shared, and for the hope that, someday, we'd meet again beyond those pearly gates.

* * *

Lenora E. Trembath is an award-winning author of *The Wisdom Answer: Equipping Teens Living in a Culture of Deception, An Interactive Journal Based on Proverbs 1-9*. With over fourteen years of homeschooling experience and a profound love for God's Word, she combines her passion for education and faith to guide readers through life's challenges.

Questions for Personal Reflection or Group Discussion

In the midst of fear and uncertainty, Lenora prayed for a moment of assurance about her father's salvation. God answered her prayer in a miraculous way as her father declared his belief in Jesus during their final conversation. Though she experienced the pain of loss, Lenora found comfort in knowing her father had embraced faith, and she treasured the memories they shared.

1. How can moments of uncertainty lead you to trust God more deeply?
2. When have you experienced God's timing in a powerful or unexpected way, especially in a difficult situation?
3. How does the assurance of a loved one's faith bring comfort in times of loss?

We pray that Lenora's story will remind you of God's faithfulness in answering prayers, even in life's most difficult moments. May it encourage you to trust that God hears and responds in His perfect timing, offering hope and comfort in the face of uncertainty. Let this story inspire you to cherish the moments you have with loved ones and to trust in God's greater plan for our lives and our eternal future.

WHEN MY STONE WAS ROLLED AWAY

BY SUSAN STEDMAN

I have been an extreme hypochondriac all my life, desperate and afraid of every physical symptom, even when they didn't exist.

On this Wednesday night in April of 2022, though, this physical symptom existed, and I was terrified. It was worse than kidney stones or childbirth. My husband took me to the hospital, and I was seen immediately. It was discovered that I had a gallstone stuck in my pancreatic duct. My liver enzymes were in the thousands, and I was septic. The doctors admitted me and planned to go down my esophagus with a scope and retrieve the stone, and then the next day remove my gallbladder. But Someone bigger than me had other plans.

I was put on a morphine drip, IV antibiotics, and electrolytes. I could have no food or liquid by mouth. My prayers were continuous. Friends and family were praying at home because I was not allowed visitors. They had been praying for me for months because I had been under mind-numbing stress to the point that I was barely functioning. My memory was affected and, obviously, my health was affected.

The doctors put me in a tiny private room, and I was able to go straight to sleep. They did not do the procedures that night or the next day. I didn't care. Things were happening that I couldn't explain. I stayed alone in that little room; the morphine drip was removed but I was given a shot every few hours for residual pain. A nurse checked on me once every four hours. I had no food or water, and I kept the lights off so that the only illumination was from the crack under the door. I never turned the TV on, I never turned my cell phone on. Sometimes I sat up in the chair, and sometimes I stretched out on the bed.

By the second day, I requested them to stop the morphine because I felt I didn't need it. The nurses were the best, in and out quietly. We shared maybe ten words a day. My friends and family were praying constantly, I was told. What I did was talk to God. Isn't that praying?

I felt that God was truly there with me the whole time, letting me lean against Him and talk. I told Him that I was sorry for being afraid to die. He laughed and said, *You always jump right to dying. What if I have you here to rest? To recover? To learn? To be quiet?* He explained death to me, that I would wake up and be near Him forever and I would never hurt again. He said that He would take care of my family. I lost a lifetime of fear of death those nights.

On Friday night, a doctor explained that my liver enzymes had returned to normal, and the stone passed on its own. They were amazed. I was finally able to have water and clear broth. While I waited for my family to come get me, I realized that I had fasted for three days, and I felt so clean and empty. Empty of awful things I'd held onto for so long. Later, I realized that I had sat alone in that dark, empty room for three days and three nights and I had come out more alive and better than ever. I was stronger, more peaceful, and happier.

I had been lifted up in prayer, and I know that God was with me, just like every day of my life.

* * *

Susan Stedman wrote her first story at six years old. She progressed to articles, essays, writing for a ministry, and has eight novels on Amazon. With years of the study of physiopsychology, her current work is about God's answers for adults who suffer the residual trauma of childhood abuse.

Questions for Personal Reflection or Group Discussion

Susan shares her profound spiritual experience during a medical crisis in April 2022. As she dealt with a gallstone that had her septic, she found herself in a small hospital room, praying and talking to God. Throughout three days and three nights of fasting, solitude, and prayer, Susan's fear of death was replaced with a sense of peace, trust in God's plan, and a deeper spiritual connection. Her story highlights the power of prayer, the importance of spiritual rest, and the transformative effect of being in God's presence during moments of trial.

1. How does Susan's journey from fear to peace inspire you to trust in God's presence and plan, especially in difficult circumstances?
2. Have you ever experienced a time when you felt God's comforting presence during a personal crisis? How did it change your perspective on the situation?
3. Susan's story highlights the idea of spiritual rest and being quiet with God. What practices can you incorporate into your life to create space for this kind of deep connection with God?

We pray that Susan's story encourages you to seek peace in God's presence during your most challenging times. Remember, as Susan experienced, that God is always with you, offering comfort, guidance, and transformation when you lean on Him in prayer.

48

ULTIMATE HEALING IN THE MIDST OF CHAOS

BY BRENT CLARK

*T*he monitors beeped steadily as David lay in bed motionless. David was not only my father-in-law but a second father and a good friend. I couldn't believe that he was fishing with his wife, Jerrie, just a month earlier, and now he was dying of cancer.

"Brent," said Jerrie, "God told Pastor Smith that David is going to live."

Pastor Smith was the visitation pastor from their church. This was confirmation to Jerrie that God was going to heal her sick husband. I had doubts, but I had seen God heal people miraculously. Jerrie, my wife, Tara, and I constantly prayed that God would heal David.

It took cancer one month to kill my father-in-law. David had suffered through inexplicable amount of pain and drugs to ease him as he slipped into eternity. I felt my heart being ripped out of my chest. It was now time for me to be a comfort to my wife and mother-in-law.

Was I angry? Sure, but not at God. I was angry at Pastor Smith for not taking God's Word seriously. Deuteronomy 18:20 says, "But the prophet who shall speak a word presumptuously in My name which I have not commanded him to speak, or which he shall speak in the name of other gods, that prophet shall die." Back in Old Testament times, false prophets were stoned to death. If someone made a prediction and spoke for God and it didn't come true, they were executed. I couldn't believe this man did this so lightly when God takes His Word so seriously.

I was completely numb at the funeral. The shock of David's passing hurt so much that I didn't know how to deal with it. I stood by Tara and held her hand as people walked by and gave their condolences. She was destroyed by grief. I didn't know how to comfort my wife as I was trying to grieve as well. I felt like there was a deep, dark hole inside of me. David and I didn't agree on various things. I came from more of a reformed background, and he a charismatic background, but his love for Jesus was obvious. I was never going to have those conversations again with him.

What was healing was the promise of Jesus Himself. Jesus said, "I am the resurrection and the life; he who believes in Me will live even if he dies" (John 11:25). David Schwendeman was a man who loved Jesus Christ. Death was the ultimate healing for him. In Heaven, there is no sickness and no suffering (Revelation 21:3-4). David is going to live forever with Christ. I am going to see him again one day.

The gospel of Jesus Christ is the most healing truth ever. We are riddled with sin, unable to save ourselves, and sin has eternal consequences. Jesus said in Matthew 25:41, "Depart from Me, accursed ones, into the eternal fire which has been prepared for the devil and his angels."

However, Scripture gives us a remedy in Jesus. He is the way, the truth, and the life, and nobody gets to the Father but through Him (John 14:6). Our response is to believe in Christ and repent of our sins. The ultimate healing is being with Jesus eternally, not being healed of sickness.

* * *

Brent Clark is a writer and photographer. He lives with his wife, Tara, in Columbus, Ohio, and is a graduate of The Ohio State University.

Questions for Personal Reflection or Group Discussion

Brent reflects on the painful loss of his father-in-law, David, who died of cancer despite fervent prayers for his healing. In the midst of this heartache, Brent wrestles with his anger, not at God, but at those who falsely assured David's family of a miraculous healing. Ultimately, Brent finds comfort in the promise of eternal life through Jesus, recognizing that David's ultimate healing came through his entrance into eternity with Christ.

1. How does Brent's journey through grief and loss challenge or deepen your understanding of healing?
2. Have you ever struggled with unanswered prayers or felt let down when a situation didn't turn out the way you hoped? How did you process those emotions?
3. What can we learn from Brent's reflection on the gospel and the ultimate healing of eternal life with Christ?

We pray that Brent's story encourages you to see that, even in the midst of sorrow and loss, God's promise of eternal life offers true and lasting healing. While physical healing may not always come, the hope of being with Christ in eternity is the greatest healing we can receive.

49

YOUR PRAYERS ARE NOT TOO SMALL FOR GOD

BY VANESSA M. JONES

I sit alone in the room, waiting, restless, in a black vinyl chair with chrome legs. I gaze at the cream-painted walls of the antiquated exam room. The silence is deafening. I anticipate the entrance and opinion of the dermatologist. He arrives with confidence and assures me he can remove the small nodule on my finger. His words are straightforward: "You will have a permanent scar."

Questions race through my mind. *Do I want a scar? Am I willing to keep the nodule?* The surge of questions continues. *If I do nothing, will it get larger? Will I have to hide my finger if it grows?* I decide to leave the nodule alone.

On my deck weeks later, the squirrels capture my attention as they run up and down the trees and across the grassy yard. The peaceful isolation from the rest of the world is delightful. Birds make beautiful music under the direction of the finest musical conductor. *God, thank You for this private concert from Your creation.* At this moment, I have everything I need—my Bible, notebook, pen, and the unseen company of my Lord.

After a time of prayer and personal Bible study, I see the unwanted nodule. *God, You are real and can do anything. Will You remove this benign growth as proof that You are listening to me? Many people are calling on You for help. Maybe I should not ask You to do this when there are needs greater than mine. I know You care about the small requests as well as the big needs. Let me see You do a miracle. You performed miracles in the past, some of them in an instance.*

I glance back at my finger. The nodule is gone. The Lord has healed me. I press on my finger several times. My examination affirms the healing. An array of expressions arise—shock, moments of stillness, excitement, and thankfulness. I look around and upward in amazement as I reflect on the goodness of my Savior.

My face is overtaken with unending smiles and unstoppable joy because of His tender touch. Happiness overwhelms me as I thank God for answering what some might consider a trivial request. I cannot wait to share this powerful miracle with my family.

The Lord gave me an extra gift that day— a faint line in place of the lump. I call it a *mark of remembrance.* Like the children of Israel who used stones to commemorate God's deliverance, I had a reminder that God listens and performs miracles.

God does not always answer my prayers in the way I want or when I prefer. I continue to pray, trust, and wait for answers. My Savior does not have to respond because I ask. And yet, He shows Himself as a faithful and trustworthy provider. He makes His love and presence known to mankind every day.

Years later, the petite, inconspicuous mark of remembrance on my finger is gone. I am proof that God hears and answers prayers —even requests that appear insignificant. No request is too small or too big for God. He knows what is best. His timing is perfect. God answers prayers His way and in His time.

Will I trust the Lord and live for Him, even if He does not respond the way I want? Yes. God is worthy of my love and worship. My devotion is not based on *if, when,* or *how* He answers my prayers. It is based on His character alone.

* * *

Vanessa M. Jones is a Bible teacher, speaker, and an award-winning writer. She writes on marriage, family, and relationships. As a contributing author, her work has appeared in regional and national publications. You can connect with her at VanessaMJones.com.

Questions for Personal Reflection or Group Discussion

Vanessa shares a powerful testimony of how God healed a small nodule on her finger, reminding her that no prayer is too small for God. Her story is a beautiful reminder that God hears even the seemingly insignificant requests and answers in His perfect way and timing. Through this experience, Vanessa is reminded to trust God, not just for the miracles, but for His faithful and loving character.

1. How does Vanessa's story encourage you to bring even your smallest requests to God in prayer?
2. Have you ever experienced a moment when God answered a prayer in a way that seemed small but deeply meaningful to you?
3. How can this story inspire you to trust in God's timing and plan, even when His answers to your prayers don't come in the way you expect?

We pray that Vanessa's story will remind you that God cares about every aspect of your life, both big and small. May it encourage you to pray boldly and trust that God listens to your heart's desires. Let this testimony inspire you to deepen your faith in God's character, knowing that He is always at work, answering prayers in His perfect way, whether they seem big or small to us.

50

UNCLE BEN

BY RALPH TURNER

I remember the Indian stamps.

Uncle Ben had been writing to me for two or three years from his mission station in south India. My parents didn't have a Christian faith and were concerned that as an impressionable eight-year-old, I would read his letters and become "religious." There was no chance of that. To this day, I only remember the stamps.

But one thing I do know: Uncle Ben was praying for me. And God answers prayer.

On a field outside St. Davids in Wales, a fifteen-year-old boy heard the gospel. It made sense. It wasn't the most emotional of responses, but that young man decided to pray. And it changed his life.

That was over fifty years ago. Many prayers have been answered since. I have a wife and a grown-up family, and every one of them acknowledges Jesus as Lord.

I have my own answered prayer stories, piled up over the years. In my Bible, I keep an email. It's from a consultant I was working with in the early 2000s. She suggested I meet her in New

York to discuss some financial issues relating to the company I was working for.

"Why don't we meet up for breakfast? There's a restaurant at the top of the two towers."

The meeting was due to take place on Tuesday morning, September 11, 2001. But there were some other things to sort out, so we postponed the meeting. And I'm here to tell the tale. And here to say that God knows our every step.

Why me? Why was I protected that day when others were not? On that day when the two towers fell? Only God knows the answer to that. But one thing I do know: God answers prayer.

Over the years, I've told that story. I've waived that piece of paper with the printed email. I've preached words of faith and declared God's blessing and protection. I've worked with an evangelistic organization and have had the privilege of seeing thousands stepping over into God's Kingdom.

God planted India in my heart. I heard Him call me to that nation, the only time I ever heard an audible word from God. My wife is from India. For a while, I thought that must be the answer —I didn't have to go to India, India had come to me! But I did go. We went together. For over twenty-five years we have had the privilege of serving the churches in India.

And it all started with a prayer.

One day, I'll get to meet Uncle Ben. I have no recollection of him, although my parents assured me that I did see him when I was small. He was so faithful in writing those letters and praying for me.

Did Uncle Ben have an inkling that God's hand was on my life? Did he know I would find life? Did he know God would call me to India? Was that the reason for his faithfulness in writing? Was that the reason he prayed for me? I had other relatives, other cousins. Maybe he wrote to them too. But one thing I am sure of: a man I don't remember meeting, living on a different continent, prayed a prayer.

God answered Uncle Ben. I am here as a result of his prayers for me. Thousands today have a living relationship with Jesus Christ as a result of his prayers for me and my response.

By my calculations, those letters were sent to me nearly sixty years ago.

I only remember the stamps. But I am so, so grateful for the prayers.

* * *

Ralph Turner is a ghostwriter of Christian autobiographies, and he also writes biographies and teaching books. His most popular book *Is There Mercy for Me?*, is the story of a hit man who died and met Jesus. Ralph is married to Rohini and part of Chroma Church in Leicester, United Kingdom.

Questions for Personal Reflection or Group Discussion

Uncle Ben faithfully prayed for his nephew, Ralph, for years, even when Ralph didn't remember much about him. Decades later, Ralph reflected on the impact of those prayers and how God used them to shape his faith and calling. Ralph's life of ministry, especially in India, and the thousands who have come to know Christ as a result, all began with the faithful prayers of a man who saw God's potential in him.

1. How does Ralph's story encourage you to pray for others, even when you don't see immediate results?
2. Have you ever experienced a time when someone's prayers made a lasting impact on your life?
3. How can you remain faithful in praying for loved ones, trusting that God is working even when you don't see the answers right away?

We pray that Ralph's story will inspire you to remain committed to praying for others, knowing that God answers prayers in ways we may never fully understand. May it encourage you to trust in the long-term impact of faithful prayer, believing that God is working through your prayers even when you don't see the immediate results. Let this testimony remind you that your prayers can plant seeds that may bear fruit for generations to come.

Made in the USA
Columbia, SC
24 November 2024

47046798R00124